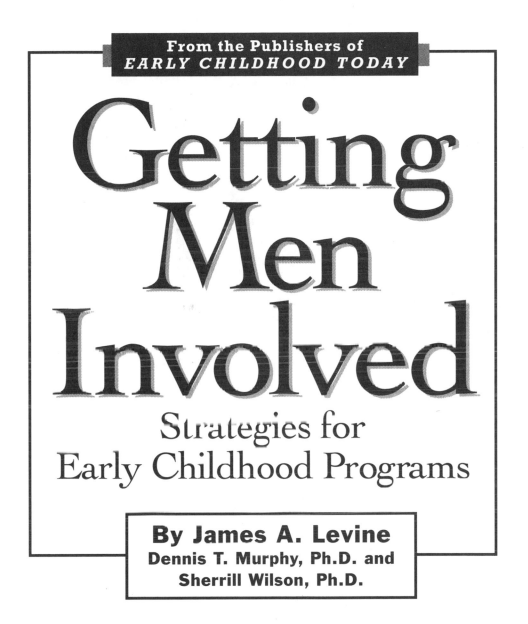

**From the Publishers of**
*EARLY CHILDHOOD TODAY*

# Getting Men Involved

## Strategies for Early Childhood Programs

### By James A. Levine
### Dennis T. Murphy, Ph.D. and
### Sherrill Wilson, Ph.D.

Child Care
Resource Network
1-800-577-2276

**Early Childhood Division Vice President and Publisher**
Helen Benham

**Editorial Director**
Julia Kristeller

**Art Director**
Mary Ann Salvato Jones

**Production Director**
Debra Ann Townes

**Editor**
Marion Lane

**Designer**
Stephanie Ingrassia

**Cover Photographs**
James Levin

Published by:
Scholastic Inc.
Early Childhood Division
730 Broadway
New York, NY 10003

ISBN # 0-590-49605-0

12, 11, 10, 9, 8, 7, 6, 5, 4, 3, 2          3, 4, 5, 6, 7, 8/9
                                                      34
Printed in the U.S.A.
First Scholastic printing, August 1993

# Contents

Acknowledgments......................5

Foreword.................................6

How To Use This Book...........7

## Rethinking Involvement

Chapter 1:.............................8
**Benefits**

Chapter 2:.............................11
**Assessing Male Involvement**

## Strategies

Chapter 3:.............................23
STAGE ONE:
**Creating a Father-Friendly Environment**

Expect Men To Be Involved

Put Out The Welcome Mat

Find Out What Men Want

Display Images of Men

Recognize the Hidden Resistance from Staff

Recognize the Hidden Resistance from Mothers

Recognize the Hidden Fears of Men

Create a Special Place for Men

Chapter 4:.............................30
STAGE TWO:
**Recruiting Men to Your Program**

The Invisible Man in the House

Bus Drivers As Recruiters

Paid Staff As Recruiters

Men As Recruiters

Women As Recruiters

Reaching Out To the Hard-to-Reach

Reaching Out To All Men

Making Dollars Talk

Chapter 5:.............................37
STAGE THREE:
**Operating a Fathers' Program**

For-Men-Only Events

Men's Work, Men's Play

Ice Breakers

Men's Groups

Activities for Men and Kids

Curriculum for Parenting

Special Recognition Events

Family Events

Skills Development

Chapter 6:.............................45
STAGE FOUR:
**Sustaining Male Involvement**

Promote the Positive

Assess Your Progress Regularly

Cultivate Your Leadership

Build a Network

**Male involvement benefits all the children in your program.**

There are many ways to keep men actively involved in your program.

# Model Programs

Chapter 7.................................**48**
**Job Training and Parent Education**
Addison County Parent-Child Center, Inc.
Middlebury, VT

Chapter 8.................................**51**
**Curriculum For Dads**
Avance
San Antonio, TX

Chapter 9.................................**54**
**Beyond the Father's Day Celebration**
Cardinal Spellman Head Start
New York, NY

Chapter 10...............................**57**
**Mentoring to Young Men**
THE CLUB
Boston, MA

Chapter 11...............................**59**
**Using the Public Schools**
Dad and Me
White Bear Lake, MN

Chapter 12...............................**62**
**The Monthly Men's Group**
Fairfax –San Anselmo Children's Center
San Rafael, CA

Chapter 13...............................**65**
**Fathers Working Together**
Florence S. Brown Pre-K Center
Rochester, NY

Chapter 14...............................**67**
**Recruiting Men**
Miami Valley Child Development Centers
Dayton, OH

Chapter 15...............................**70**
**Male Involvement Specialists**
The Ounce of Prevention Fund
Chicago, IL

Chapter 16...............................**72**
**Reaching Fathers at Home**
Parents As Teachers
St. Louis, MO

Chapter 17...............................**74**
**Bus Drivers As Recruiters**
Parents in Community Action
Minneapolis, MN

Chapter 18...............................**78**
**Reaching Men From the Community**
Pinebelt Association For
Community Enhancement
Hattiesburg, MS

Chapter 19...............................**80**
**The Men's Group**
St. Bernadines Head Start
Baltimore, MD

Chapter 20:...............................**84**
**Reaching Men on the Move**
Texas Migrant Council
Laredo, TX

Resources...............................**86**
Books For Children,
Materials for Professionals and Parents,
and Organizations

About This Book..................**95**

About the Authors.................**96**

# Acknowledgments

This book wouldn't have been possible without generous assistance from many people, and we'd like to thank them all:

**Our Funders:** The Smith Richardson and A.L. Mailman Foundations provided the financial support that made our research possible. Thanks to their boards and staffs, and especially to Elizabeth Marx and Luba Lynch.

**Our Advisors:** Project consultant Joan Lombardi has helped at virtually every stage of this project. Members of our distinguished Advisory Panel have provided input at different points along the way. Thanks to Carrie Cheek, Hector DeLeon, Sarah Greene, Arvern Moore, Lynne Pooley, Doug Powell, Kyle Pruett, Gloria Rodriguez, Maurice Sykes, Heather Weiss, Les Willis, Arnold Yazzi, and Jim Young. And thanks to Ed Zigler, who has been an advocate for our work from the beginning.

**Programs:** Directors, staffs, and parents at all the programs profiled gave generously of their time. This book is really our translation of their work. Special thanks to the following and the teams they work with: Mary Sue Bennett, Peggy Butler, Isaac Cardenas, Alyce Dillon, Adama Ekulona, Sue Harding, Lowell Johnson, Janet McElrath, Joanne Milano, Cheryl Mitchell, Bryan Nelson, Gay Newsome, Jay Ostrower, Blas Reyes, Lisa Russell, Stan Seiderman, Jeanette Taylor, Marilyn Thomas, Clarence Tucker, Sheila Tucker, Roy Turner, Hector Villarreal, and Mildred Winter. We also conducted telephone interviews with many programs and visited many others that we did not profile. Thanks to all of them.

**Colleagues:** Many colleagues at the Families and Work Institute and elsewhere gave us input and support in developing this work. Special thanks to Emily Coplon, Glen DeLaMota, Arielle Eckstut, Dana Friedman, Ellen Galinsky, Rick Johnson, Michael Lamb, Julie Levine, Glen Palm, Joseph Pleck, Darryl Reaves, Tanya Rivera, Melissa Rowland, Laura Sedlock, Al Smith, and Edie Stern. And an extra thanks to Ann Stell for developing the bibliography of children's books.

**Publisher:** At Scholastic, Helen Benham and Marion Lane gave us good editorial advice for tightening this manuscript; Mary Ann Salvato Jones joined our team just in time to provide art direction.

**Family:** All of our families put up with lots of travel on this one! Thanks to Joan, Diane, Andrew, Jennifer, and Sherrill for your patience and good cheer.

# Foreword

It was 1968 and I was dressed as the Great Pumpkin.

To the 20 preschoolers gathered at my knee, it wasn't an unusual sight: it was circle time at Halloween and I was their teacher.

To the children's parents it was very unusual. "What do you really do?" they wanted to know.

It was a question that never would have been asked of a woman. My female colleagues could work with three-and four-year-olds all their lives without anybody expecting they should or might be doing something else. But a man spending so much time with young children?

That moment a quarter of a century ago changed my view of the world. It shocked me into realizing that gender stereotypes affect men, as well as women. Intellectually, of course, I knew that such stereotyping was widespread, affecting all sorts of other people. But this was deeply personal. People didn't expect me to teach or care for young children.

It was a challenge to my very identity. I had always been interested in kids and teaching came naturally to me. My own teachers in elementary and high school recognized that and asked me to tutor students who were having difficulty. In college, I volunteered to work with grade school children whose families couldn't afford tutoring. In my spare time, I began reading books about child psychology and the phenomenal amount of learning that takes place in the early years. So, teaching preschoolers in East Oakland, California, was a job that seemed made for me.

Five years later, as a consultant on children's programs to The Ford Foundation, I ran smack into the same assumptions about men and realized this had implications far beyond my ego. A group of us had been asked to advise the Foundation on how to spend its money to affect child care and social policy. Underlying all our recommendations was one principle: child care was a women's problem and women were its solution. Some experts recommended investing in group care, where women working in centers would care for other women's children. Others advocated family care, where women in their own homes would care for other women's children. Men were invisible.

Buoyed by my training as the Great Pumpkin—and by then I was also the father of a two-year-old—I turned to the group and said: "I think we've got this all wrong. We will never find a solution to child care if we keep defining it as a women's issue instead of a family issue. Don't men have an interest in children? Don't they have responsibilities for them? Aren't they fathers? Can't they be child care workers? Why do we keep assuming they don't exist?"

Since that time, I have been conducting research designed to reframe the way our society thinks and acts about men's role in child rearing. Under the auspices of The Fatherhood Project, which I founded in 1981 at the Bank Street College of Education and relocated in 1989 to the Families and Work Institute, my colleagues and I have been examining the future of fatherhood, as well as ways to support men's involvement in the education and care of children. This book on early childhood programs is just one part of a broad research program that is examining how all our social systems—including the workplace, social services, and the law—affect men's connection to kids. In over a decade's research, we were struck by two findings within the early childhood community: Although many programs said they wanted to get men more involved, they simply didn't know how — despite repeated efforts, nothing worked. Yet, at the same time, a small but increasing number of programs seemed to be figuring out innovative ways to do just that.

Thanks to support from the Smith Richardson and A.L. Mailman Foundations, we've been able to visit some of those innovative programs, learn what makes them work, and pass their "best practices" on to you. Although we've emphasized programs serving low-income families, the lessons learned in our research will be valuable to all programs.

As you read this book, think of yourself as entering into a national dialogue, joining a community of practitioners who are also trying to get men involved.

—BY JAMES A. LEVINE

James A. Levine, as a preschool teacher, with his daughter Jessica, now 23 years old.

# How to Use This Book

## Approaching Male Involvement in Your Program

This book is designed to offer you a systematic way of thinking about and approaching male involvement. The first section will help you understand why male involvement is important, assess the extent of its existence at your program, and set goals for the future.

In the second section we provide specific strategies, many of which you can implement right away. While you can dip in anywhere and find them useful, the strategies are carefully organized into a four-stage process that we found implicit across successful programs.

Next, we will introduce you to fourteen exemplary model programs, representing a broad racial, ethnic, and geographic mix. If you read about a strategy and wonder how it looks and feels as part of a program you can find it in these models.

Finally, we are including a comprehensive set of resources for you to use in developing your curriculum and program.

## Becoming Part of a National Dialogue

*Getting Men Involved* is just one piece of The Fatherhood Project's ongoing effort to spread good ideas for practice throughout the early childhood community. You can be part of that effort. If you have developed strategies for involving men that you think should be brought to national attention, let us know. If you know of programs that should be recognized as national models, let us know. And if you are encountering resistance in your efforts to involve men, we want to hear about that too; it's as important to learn from problems as from successes.

We will help translate your input to the rest of the early childhood community in several ways. We will incorporate it into our workshops and presentations. And we will use it to enrich one of our latest initiatives, a National Training and Technical Assistance Project on Male Involvement. We hope you will want to join with other early childhood professionals in this effort. You can share your ideas and get on our mailing list for future announcements by writing to:

**The Fatherhood Project**
**Families and Work Institute**
**330 Seventh Avenue**
**New York City, NY 10001**

# Rethinking Involvement

How men relate to children is influenced by how they think and feel about their role and how others perceive them.

## CHAPTER ① Benefits

If you want to get men more involved in your program, and need help getting started, this book is for you! When we use the words "father" or "men" in this book, we mean any significant male in a child's life. This could be an uncle, grandfather, mother's friend, volunteer from the community, as well as a biological, step, or adoptive father.

Why should you want to get men more involved? This chapter provides an overview of the benefits to children, to families, and to your program, along with some of the most common questions asked about getting men involved.

### Benefits for Children

What do we know about the impact of getting men more involved? Strictly speaking, very little. However, we can get an inkling of the impact of increased male involvement by extrapolating from studies of the father's influence in child rearing. These consistently show that it is not the mere presence of males that has an effect, but the way they interact with children.

■ **Sex-Role Development.** Research has consistently shown that a warm and nurturing relationship with the father helps children grow up feeling comfortable with whatever society has currently determined as appropriate behavior for men and women. It's the nature of that relationship — not the masculinity of the father — that affects his children. Male involvement does not help boys become "real men" or girls become "real women" in a narrow or tradition-ally-stereotyped way.

■ **Social Adjustment.** A long line of studies has tried to establish a relationship between father absence and juvenile delinquency. It is not clear, however, whether juvenile delinquency can be attributed to fatherlessness, the conditions under which the father left, or low family income (which often results directly from father absence). Research does suggest, however, that it is not just availability of the father, but his style of interaction that has an effect. Boys and girls with involved and nurturant fathers tend to be better adjusted.

■ **Cognitive Development.** Recent studies in which fathers provide at least 40 percent of the within-family care for preschoolers show increased cognitive competence as well as more empathy and less sex-stereotyped beliefs. Again, however, it is not just the father's presence but his nurturing manner that has positive consequences.

The research on father involvement has important implications for early childhood programs. It suggests that programs can make a positive contribution by helping fathers — or other men — develop a warm, comfortable relationship with their children. And it suggests that *how* men relate to children is influenced by how they think and feel about their role, how others perceive them, and whether or not they have a support system.

Boiled down, this means: Children benefit from warm and nurturing relationships with men, and men are most likely to develop those sorts of relationships in environments which value, support, and encourage them. As a kind of shorthand, we call such settings "father-friendly environments." The next section of this book will show you how to create and sustain father-friend-ly environments.

## What About Single Parent Families?
One of the most frequent worries early childhood professionals have about efforts to increase male involvement is that it will be hurtful to the large number of preschool children growing up in sin-gle parent female-headed households—that it will highlight the absence of fathers in their lives. Isn't it better to just leave things as they are?

First let's be clear about purposes and assump-tions: increasing male involvement in or via early childhood programs will not solve the problem of single parenthood in America. But that's no rea-

son to see it as harmful. Watch what happens when a man walks into virtually any preschool classroom anywhere in the country; he is like a walking magnet, with some invisible force pulling children onto his back and legs.

There is an enormous amount of father hunger among children in America: children who don't have a father living at home as well as children whose father's work limits their contact. Getting more men involved in your program won't restore the missing father in these children's lives. However, it will help replace a very limited idea of fatherhood — a vague abstraction or a stereo-typed image taken from television — with a con-crete and fuller sense of nurturant manhood. As you'll see in our sections on strategies and mod-els, the men you get involved in your program can be available to all the children.

## What About Cultural Differences?
What about cultures that only consider it appro-priate for women to care for children? Is it possi-ble to balance cultural sensitivity with equality or opportunity for men and women?

If you think you're working with a group that's not receptive to the notion of male involve-ment, consider the situation of two Head Start trainers trying to promote male involvement to Inuit tribes in remote villages of Alaska. It was about as easy as selling, as the old joke has it, ice-boxes to Eskimos. According to one Inuit custom, a man cannot take the risk of holding a young child who is not toilet trained or who might have an "accident" on him. The reason: the scent of urine will spoil the hunt, since it lets animals smell the hunter approaching. The fact that most Inuit men hunt for sport rather than subsistence does not seem to matter very much. The men in

**Boys and girls with involved and nurturant fathers tend to be better adjusted.**

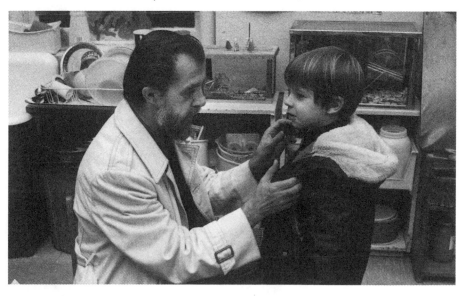

ERIKA STONE

The stereotype that women alone should care for children limits the opportunities and talents of both sexes.

these villages don't expect to have much direct contact with their children—typically their sons—until they are old enough to join in the hunt.

Add to this situation that the two Head Start trainers are women and you can see just how difficult it was. The trainers were outraged that Eskimo women were being put in the position of having to do all the child care because of the antiquated hunting myth. They sincerely wanted to promote male involvement for children and their fathers. And they had been taught just how important it is to respect cultural differences, not to automatically impose their values.

Or consider the case of a predominantly Mexican-American early childhood program in Texas. After the director, who is a man, hired a male teacher to work in the three-year-old classroom, he ran into an unforeseen problem. The mothers stopped coming to parent meetings because their husbands prevented them; the husbands didn't want their wives to be with this "other man." So in his efforts to break down a stereotype by having a man in the classroom, this director ran smack into another stereotype: the jealously of Hispanic machismo.

In each of these cases, it would have been easy for the early childhood professionals to say "they're wrong," to assert their professionalism over the local culture. But to do so would have alienated the very group they were trying to get involved. It simply wouldn't have worked.

Neither the trainers in Alaska nor the director in Texas gave up their goals. They recognized the strength of the local culture and adopted a different strategy: education. In each case they held meetings to explain the benefits of male involvement for children. Without forcing their views on the parent body, they started a process of broadening their views. Without directly challenging the culture, they offered an alternative. And in each case, they greatly modified their timetable for change, realizing that acceptance would take longer than they originally thought.

No doubt you will face situations where culture is at odds with the goal of male involvement. If you don't show your respect for the culture, you'll lose your constituency. But that

doesn't mean you have to give up the long-term goal of male involvement. With an educational approach to change, you can find a balance that will work over a longer timetable.

## Benefits For Women

While doing our national search for exemplary programs, we received a call from a woman who directs a preschool program in Kansas. "I've heard about your project," she said, "and I just don't understand why anybody would want to get more men involved. All our teachers are women, and we're doing just fine."

In calling for greater male involvement we're not suggesting that women aren't doing or can't do a good job. But in the long run, we believe it's healthier for our society — and for women — to encourage both men and women to be involved with the care and education of young children.

The stereotype that women alone should care for children — or that they alone are capable of caring for children—limits the opportunities and talents of both sexes. It places the burden on women to stay home with children, and keeps men from the joys of closer involvement as fathers. It leads women disproportionately into the "caring" professions without exploring a broader set of career options, and it keeps men from broadening their career options to include the "caring" professions, despite their interests or abilities. Moreover, it perpetuates the devaluation of both women and children, linking them together in a "feminine" world that is deemed less serious and important the the world of "masculine" activities.

Our society is beginning to recognize both the inevitability and the value of racial and cultural diversity. But another dimension of diversity is valuing the interests and talents of both sexes, of recognizing the contributions that both women and men can make to children, and to one another in their work with children.

Inevitably there will be resistance from women about getting men more involved, resistances that some women may have a hard time acknowledging. Many women have had bad personal experiences with men. They have been abandoned or abused — as children and as adults.

As men get more involved in early childhood programs, there will be tensions between men and women that neither anticipated. But there will also be new opportunities for dialogue and understanding. In an imperfect world, the early childhood classroom allows us to create a microcosm of what we would like the world to be.

**A large part of male involvement consists of the little things that happen every day.**

CHAPTER

# Assessing Male Involvement

What do we mean by involvement? How does it show up in your program? Consider the "before" and "after" table on page 12 drawn from programs that made an effort to reach men.

You'd probably agree that each of these examples—except, perhaps, the last—describe an instance of male involvement. The last example may seem too informal to you, not nearly a specific enough activity to qualify as male involvement. We think that it's one of the most important; hold on and we'll return to it soon!

The point of these examples is that male involvement is not one thing; it is the accumulated and ongoing set of behaviors or actions that, taken together, reflects the tone or feeling of your program and its relationship to men.

## What's Your Attitude?

Try this quick quiz. Over the course of a day or so, ask 10 people in your program—they can be staff, parents, or board members—the following three questions:

1) **Are you in favor of parent involvement?**
2) **Are you in favor of involvement by fathers and other men?**
3) **What would our program look like if we were successful at involving men?**

It is likely that most people you ask will answer "yes" to questions one and two. However, it would not surprise us if the responses to ques-

*JAMES LEVIN*

| Before | After |
|---|---|
| **Four-year-old Jamal waits** with his mother on the corner for the big, yellow Head Start bus. | **Jamal waits with his mom's boyfriend, Derek.** Once a month Derek is the "parent volunteer rider," staying on the bus while it picks up all the other kids. At the center, Derek visits in Jamal's classroom for about an hour before the bus driver gives him a lift back home. |
| **When it is time for the monthly Parent Council meeting,** Hector drives his wife, Dolores, to the center. While she attends the meeting, he stays in his pick-up truck listening to the radio. | **Hector and Dolores attend the meeting together.** Hector still mostly listens, but he and Delores discuss the meeting together, on the way home. |
| **Everyday Mr. Chung drives his daughter, Kim, to the center.** She hops out of the car and runs down the walk; once inside the gate, she waves and he drives off. | **Mr. Chung still doesn't come into the center too often,** but he leads the twice-a-year family camping outing where he gets to meet most of the children and parents. |
| **Four-year-old Ernestine tells** the other kids that she doesn't have a daddy. | **Ernestine tells the other kids her daddy doesn't live with her** and sometimes it makes her sad. But she also tells them about Mr. Jones from the Army base, who does woodworking with her at the center once a week. |
| **When he picks his son, T.J., up at the center,** Mr. Thomas doesn't initiate conversation with the staff about what T.J. has been doing and the staff doesn't realize that he is curious but uncomfortable. | **Mr. Thomas is always greeted by at least one teacher.** He is openly amazed and grateful to hear about all the things T.J. is doing, and all the things going on at the center. |

tion three varied widely.

There is widespread agreement that parent involvement is beneficial to early childhood programs. However, there is no uniform definition of exactly what parent involvement is and how much of it there should be.

When it comes to male involvement, disagreement about definition is compounded by the doubt that anything will be able to get them involved.

What's the attitude among the staff in your program? And if you succeeded in getting men involved, what would your program look like?

## Assessing Your Program

To help you assess your program and set goals, we have developed the Male Involvement Profile. The Profile includes five broad categories: *Communication, Education, Other Activities, Decision-making,* and *Self-development.*

In each category, a series of questions asks you to think about *what* you are doing to involve men — specific activities and behaviors. Another set of questions asks you *how* you're doing it. *How* is just as important as *what*.

For each program area, the Profile asks you to rate yourself on both the whats and the hows. By averaging your scores across areas, you can get your overall program rating. The rating scale is:

- ■ 1  **Haven't even thought about it.**
- ■ 2  **Good intentions, but haven't done much.**
- ■ 3  **Beginning to work seriously on male involvement.**
- ■ 4  **Working actively in some areas.**
- ■ 5  **Working actively in all areas.**

The ready-to-use Profile appears on pages 17-21. To show you how to complete the Profile, and to explain how it interacts with other parts of this book, a sample Profile with completed questions from each of its five categories, follows. The answers are from a program we'll call ABC.

### Communication

The lifeline of any organization is communication, how well people are listened to and heard. If parents feel they are being paid attention to and have a chance to speak up, they will feel involved. But often early childhood communication systems are designed—albeit unintentionally — to promote interaction between female parents and female staff.

ABC doesn't exclude men in any way. Its *what* column shows that all parents *are* welcome, and that it might want to stretch its thinking about who else to invite. It is possible that men really aren't available to this program. But the *how* column suggests that their unavailability might be related, at least in part, to the way

## Parent-Teacher Meetings

| | What do you do? | | How do you do it? | 1–5 Rating |
|---|---|---|---|---|
| **Does the father of the child—or another significant male—participate at formally scheduled parent-teacher meetings?** | We invite the parents but we hardly ever get a father showing up. It never occurred to us to ask the mother if there was another important male figure in the child's life and if she wanted him to attend. | **Do you actively and continuously encourage him to participate? Do you encourage some men but not others? How comfortable do you feel about encouraging male involvement?** | At the beginning of the year we tell families that we'd like mothers and fathers to attend. We don't keep reminding them that we'd like to see fathers. By now we sort of assume that the men aren't available. | 2 |
| **What message or value statement do you think your parent-teacher meetings communicate to families about the male role?** | That men aren't available. That moms can do it alone. That it's not our place to intrude. | **When mothers and fathers are present, do you talk to both equally? Do you assume mothers care more about their children than fathers?** | We talk to both, but we emphasize communication with the mother, since she's usually more available. We do assume that mothers care more, but we've never really discussed it as a staff or with our parent group. | 2 |

ABC's welcome message is being sent.

There are four dimensions of *how* to keep in mind as you complete your Profile:

■ **Activity:** Are you working actively and consciously to make things happen, or are you in a passive mode, letting things happen only if parents initiate them?

■ **Reach:** Does a small core group—a set of regulars — always get involved, or is participation broadbased? You may want to extend your reach; to get men to extend themselves, you may have to do some extending too.

■ **Continuity:** Do you keep at it, or do you actively reach out once or twice, perhaps at the beginning of the year and when Father's Day comes around?

■ **Comfort:** How comfortable are you about encouraging male involvement? And how comfortable are men about the ways they are involved? If you answer these questions honestly, you'll get very useful information. You may identify some hidden barriers and open yourself to change and growth.

In the parent-teacher meetings example above, the *how* column reveals that ABC isn't extending its welcome very actively or continuously. In its self-rating for this section, ABC

## Daily Drop-Off and Pick-Up

| | What do you do? | | How do you do it? | Rating |
|---|---|---|---|---|
| **What type of communication occurs with parents at the beginning or end of the day?** | We try to tell parents about anything special that their child did or said. We like to tell parents good things but if we have a worry—like maybe a child is getting sick—we always mention that. It's pretty busy and we're often rushed. | **Do staff approach mothers and fathers differently? Do staff feel more comfortable approaching some men rather than others? Do some staff members feel more comfortable than others in speaking with men?** | All our staff are women and they're definitely more comfortable talking to mothers. There are one or two fathers that people tend to speak to—they're the friendly, outgoing ones. And Susan and Jan are the ones who tend to talk to them. | 3 |
| **How often during a week is there conversation between staff and a significant male? How often is there conversation about a significant male?** | Maybe twice a week. We don't talk too much about the fathers in our staff meetings. | **Do mothers and fathers seem equally comfortable approaching staff? Do some men seem more comfortable than others in speaking to staff?** | The mothers are definitely more comfortable. There are a couple of guys who are friendly, but the others sort of come and go without saying much. We assume they're busy or not interested, but maybe they're uncomfortable and don't know what to say to us. | 2 |

scored itself consistently at level 2. Since this program had thought of itself as really trying to reach men, seeing that number was a wake-up call: It had good intentions, but hadn't done much about them yet.

By answering a set of questions about drop-off and pick-up in the Communication section of the Profile on page 13, ABC learned even more:

The *what* column shows that ABC is trying to make daily contact with parents, but the *how* column suggests the need for a staff discussion. Why is it that only two staff members really feel comfortable extending themselves to men? And what might account for the fact that only a few men seem comfortable when they pick their children up?

In case you're used to thinking of parent involvement as what goes on at formally organized meetings instead of the informal chit-chat at drop-off and pickup time, you should know about Dr. Douglas Powell's provocative study of relations between parents and staff in early childhood programs. Powell discovered that "the highest frequency of communication between parents and caregivers occurred at the 'transition point' when parents left and retrieved their child at the center. Some 66% of parents reported discussions with caregivers during this transiting time on a weekly or more frequent basis" (Powell, 1989, p. 61). This type of communication was far more regular than parent-teacher conferences, which were infrequent at best and not used at all by 25 percent of the parents. Moreover, as frequency of communication increased, so did the diversity of topics — moving from exclusive focus on the child to include information related to parents and family. A further study of parent-staff communication at transition points identified them as an important way for teachers to provide "informal parent education" (Powell &

Stremmel, 1987).

Powell's studies point to an important and typically overlooked dimension of parent involvement. It may be that what happens with parents at naturally occurring transition points — or whenever communication can occur naturally — is as important as any of the more formal and programmatic aspects of parent involvement. Daily drop-off and pick-up, as well as other transition points, provide a continuing stream of opportunities to hook men into your program.

## Education

No matter how good your communication is with parents, they achieve a different level of understanding when they actually spend time with their children in your program — when they see and feel what goes on at the water table or in the blocks area or on the playground. Men often hear about these things secondhand, through the staff members or their wives. But it doesn't have to be that way. Take a look at some questions about your classroom (see below) from the Profile.

In this case, the *what* column shows that ABC, like many programs, concentrates much of its effort to reach men around one event or one time of the year, the third week in June. The *how* column shows that it also concentrates most of the responsibility for reaching men on one person, the director. That may be a heavy load to carry whether you're trying to reach women or men. When ABC examined its responses here and in other parts of the Profile, it saw the need to spread it's male involvement activities across more time and more people.

## Other Program Activities

There are many facets of your program that offer opportunities for parents to participate. While it's desirable for parents to spend time in

| Classroom | What do you do? | | How do you do it? | Rating |
|---|---|---|---|---|
| **Are parents always welcome to visit the classroom? Do you have a regularly scheduled program of parent participation that includes the significant males in children's lives? Do you have a program to bring men from the community in as volunteers?** | Parents can make appointments to visit, they can't just drop in. We always invite both parents, but don't get many men showing up – except at Father's Day when we have our yearly event to acknowledge and welcome men. We've limited this to men in the family. We haven't thought about opening things up to the community. | **Do you actively and continuously encourage the participation of men? With them directly or through their female partners? Do you expect all men to participate or just some? Do you encourage all men or just some? Does all the staff do the encouraging?** | We assume that if we invite mothers, they'll tell fathers — if there's a father around. Usually it's the director's job to encourage the parents; we haven't shared that responsibility as a full staff. Our expectations aren't too high. | 2 |

## Transportation

| | What do you do? | | How do you do it? | Rating |
|---|---|---|---|---|
| If you have a bus or van system, do you require parents to take turns riding? Do you ask fathers as well as mothers to help out? | We've never required parents to do that. It's an interesting idea, but I'm not sure how we could make it work. | How well does your transportation staff know the community—and the men in children's lives? When you review individual children's behavior, do you ask for input from your drivers? | Some of our drivers have a very good sense of the community. Since most of them are men, maybe they do know what's going on with other men. We haven't really asked them. And as for observing the kids, they're not really trained. | 1 |

the classroom, they can also stay connected to the program in other ways as well. This section of the Profile gives you some to consider, such as transportation (above).

ABC, like most programs, hasn't thought much about the link between transportation and male involvement. The Strategies and Model Programs in the rest of this book will show how that link can be made. At Minnesota's Parents in Community Action, for example, bus drivers are a key component of outreach to men and an integral part of the educational staff.

### Decision Making

Being able to influence the direction of your program is an important way for parents to be involved. Sometimes men shy away from this type of involvement because they feel unprepared. This section of the Profile will help you examine key areas of decision making, such as parent advisory councils (below).

ABC's response brings to the surface an issue that lurks in many programs. Often the assumption is made that men will only get involved if they have positions of power. The Profile will lead ABC to have a discussion of its assumptions about how to reach men, and of how men and women can work together.

### Self-Development Activities

By offering opportunities for parents to devel-op skills or knowledge, you increase their sense of engagement with your program and increase the chances that they will get involved in other ways as well. Often, however, because men are not as readily available, these opportunities are made available to women, not to men. Parent education is one example of self-development activities from the Profile (see page 16).

ABC's answer shows that despite its good intentions at reaching parents, it is assuming it can reach fathers in exactly the same way that it reaches mothers. By reading our Strategies it will discover that often the most effective outreach to men, at least initially, is through social events that have nothing to do with parenting.

The Male Involvement Profile on pages 17-21 is an effective tool that helps stimulate reflection and discussion about your program. Photocopy it and make it available for staff or parent meetings as a basis for group discussion and planning. You can also use the Profile to assess your progress: keep the copies you fill out now and compare them to copies you'll fill out later.

The Profile can also be used to assess your overall parent involvement activities. Our emphasis on male involvement is not intended to slight parent involvement in general or mothers in particular; indeed, it's women who usually are more involved. Our goal with this Profile is to shift your perspective. In doing so, you'll be

## Parent Advisory Councils

| | What do you do? | | How do you do it? | Rating |
|---|---|---|---|---|
| Do you have male representation on your parent advisory council, board of directors, or other governing body? | The vice president of our council is a man. It's the first time we've had a man in that position. | Do you actively cultivate interest among men about serving? Do you tend to give men important board positions just because they are men? How does your staff feel about this? | This guy expressed some interest so after a few months we made him vice president. Actually, the women on the staff are resentful. Why should he all of a sudden get an important position when he hasn't done anything before? | 3 |

| Parent Education | | What do you do? | | How do you do it? | Rating |
|---|---|---|---|---|---|
| Do you offer any program or services to help parents deal with the challenges of childrearing? Are any of these activities geared specifically for fathers? | | We have occasional speakers in our child development series. We invite everybody, but few men attend. We've never had a speaker just for the fathers. | Do you make specific efforts to encourage men to attend? How do you know you are addressing the particular concerns that men have? | We don't do any specific outreach to the men. We assume if we tell the mothers, they'll tell the fathers. And what specific concerns might men have? | 2 |

taking steps to encourage the involvement of both mothers and fathers.

## How Much is Enough?

You may be wondering if there is a certain minimum level of male involvement that your program should have.

Unfortunately, there is no single right way, no formula that will make your program successful. There are no cookie cutters here. Each program has to chart it's own way.

But implicit in the Male Involvement Profile are some principles and goals to work toward:

**A key to successful male involvement is creating an environment in which men as well as women are expected to be involved.**

active over passive approaches; informal opportunities for communication as much as formal programming; continuing activities more than incidental ones, although there will certainly be occasions when you hold an event only one time or once a year; a comfortable, unforced environment for male involvement over one where things are done "because we're supposed to"; and approaches that reach a broader rather than a narrower group of men.

Given these principles, which program would you think is more successful at getting men involved, the one at which 50 percent of the fathers attend and sit passively through an annual policy meeting or the one at which 20 percent of fathers have become accustomed to lively exchanges every other day with their child's teachers? Although both show progress and both need work, we'd choose the latter. We'd want to find out why the men in the first program are passive and move them towards active engagement; in the second, we'd want to reach the other 80 percent!

Successful male involvement doesn't require a specific program. If the Fairfax-San Anselmo Children's Center, which you'll read about in chapter 12, took away the Men's Group it's been operating for over a decade, it would still have significant male involvement: fathers would attend parent-teacher meetings as frequently as mothers; there would still be male staff in every classroom, including the infant program; and the visual cues in the environment would still give out the message that men are very welcome.

The keys to successful male involvement appear to be creating an environment in which men as well as women are expected to be involved; in which there is a genuine receptivity to parents, and in which there are some male staff on board.

Now you have a tool to assess where you are and to give you some ideas about where you want to go. Now we will move on to practical strategies for involving men.

ERIKA STONE

# Male Involvement Profile

| Rating Guide | |
|---|---|
| Haven't even thought about it | 1 |
| Good intentions, but haven't done much | 2 |
| Beginning to work seriously on male involvement | 3 |
| Working actively in some areas | 4 |
| Working actively in all areas | 5 |

(Fill in the boxes and rate yourself on each section. Take your average rating at the end of each category.)

Name_____ Program _____

## Communication

### Parent Teacher Meetings

| | What do you do? | | How do you do it? | Rating |
|---|---|---|---|---|
| Does the father of the child--or another significant male-participate at formally scheduled parent-teacher meetings? | | Do you actively and continuously encourage him to participate? Do you encourage some men but not others? How comfortable do you feel about encouraging male involvement? | | |
| What message or values statement do your parent-teacher meetings communicate to families about the male's role? | | When mothers and fathers are present, do you talk to both equally? Do you assume mothers care more about their children than fathers? | | |

### Written Announcements

| | What do you do? | | How do you do it? | Rating |
|---|---|---|---|---|
| Are announcements addressed to "mother" or to "parents?" If the father is not living in the home, is he sent announcements of program activities? Is any important male invited to attend? | | How active is your effort to reach men? Do you assume they are available? Do you assume they are unavailable? Do you assume the mother doesn't want him involved? Have you discussed this with her? | | |

### Special Events

| | What do you do? | | How do you do it? | Rating |
|---|---|---|---|---|
| When you have pot-luck dinners, family outings, or celebrations, do fathers or other significant males attend? What type of communication goes on between parents and staff at these events? | | Do you actively and continuously solicit the participation of men at these events? Do staff members relate differently to mothers and fathers? | | |

**Daily Drop-Off and Pick-Up**

| | What do you do? | | How do you do it? | Rating |
|---|---|---|---|---|
| **What type of communication occurs with parents at the beginning of the day?** | | **Do staff approach mothers and fathers differently?** <br><br> **Do staff feel more comfortable approaching some men rather than others?** <br><br> **Do some staff members feel more comfortable than others in speaking with men?** | | |
| **How often during a week is there a conversation between staff and a significant male?** | | **Do mothers and fathers seem equally comfortable approaching staff?** <br> **Do some men seem more comfortable than others in speaking to staff?** <br> **Are there certain staff members men feel particularly comfortable talking to?** | | |
| **If children ride the bus, does the driver have regular contact with parents? With fathers — or a significant male — as well as with mothers?** | | **Do you think of the drivers as part of your family support staff?** <br><br> **Do your drivers think of themselves that way?** <br> **How much discussion have you had about their role in your program?** | | |

**Average Rating_____**
(Add your ratings in this category and divide by 7)

# Participation in Child's Education

**Classroom**

| | What do you do? | | How do you do it? | Rating |
|---|---|---|---|---|
| **Are parents welcome to visit the classroom?** <br><br><br> **Do you have a regularly scheduled program of parent participation that includes the significant males in children's lives?** <br> **Do you have a program to bring men from the community in as volunteers?** | | **Do you actively and continuously encourage the participation of males?** <br> **Directly with them or through their female partners?** <br><br> **Do you expect all men to participate or just some?** <br><br> **Do you encourage all men or just some?** <br><br> **Does all the staff do the encouraging?** | | |

## Home Visiting

| | What do you do? | | How do you do it? | Rating |
|---|---|---|---|---|
| Does your program make home visits? Does it schedule them when both parents — or mother and a significant male — are available? | | How actively do you work to determine if there is a signifi-cant male in the child's life? | | |

## Field Trips

| | What do you do? | | How do you do it? | Rating |
|---|---|---|---|---|
| When you enlist parent volunteers as chaper-ones, do you seek men as well as women?<br><br>Do you ask parents — including men — to sug-gest field trips, including places where they work or places of interest in the community? | | How actively do you seek men for these trips?<br><br>How comfortable do staff members feel about having them along?<br><br>Do you feel comfortable having men take children to the bathroom on field trips? | | |

**Average Rating** _____
(Add your ratings in this category and divide by 3)

# Other Program Activities

## Transportation

| | What do you do? | | How do you do it? | Rating |
|---|---|---|---|---|
| If you have a bus or van system, do you require parents to take turns rid-ing? Do you ask fathers as well as mothers to help out? | | How well does your trans-portation staff know the community—and the men in children's lives? When you review individual children's behavior, do you ask for input from your drivers? | | |

## Maintenance

| | What do you do? | | How do you do it? | Rating |
|---|---|---|---|---|
| Do you have a regularly scheduled program for parents to fix up or do odd jobs at your center? Do you make a special point to ask dads and other men to help out? | | How actively and continu-ously do you reach out to involve men in mainte-nance? How comfortable does staff feel having men around to help out? | | |

## Food Services

| | What do you do? | | How do you do it? | Rating |
|---|---|---|---|---|
| Are there opportunities for parents to join their children at lunch or snack time?<br><br>Do you invite dads as well as moms? | | How actively do you seek men's participation?<br><br>Do you keep going back to the same few, or do you reach out to men who haven't participated? | | |

**Average Rating**_____
(Add your ratings in this category and divide by 3)

# Decision Making

## Parent Advisory Councils

| | What do you do? | | How do you do it? | Rating |
|---|---|---|---|---|
| Do you have male representation on your parent advisory council, board of directors, or other governing body? | | Do you actively cultivate interest among men in serving?<br><br>Do you tend to give men important board positions just because they are men? How does your staff feel about this? | | |

## Representation

| | What do you do? | | How do you do it? | Rating |
|---|---|---|---|---|
| Do you send members of the parent body or staff to regional or national meetings?<br><br>Do you include fathers or other men as representatives? | | How actively do you try to include men?<br><br>Do you save the "best" assignments for men, because you think that's the only way you can involve them? | | |

## Special Committees

| | What do you do? | | How do you do it? | Rating |
|---|---|---|---|---|
| Do you form special committees for staff hiring, fundraising, or other activities? Do you include male representation? | | How actively do you seek men's involvement?<br>Do you tend to rely on the same few over and over, or do you seek new participants? | | |

**Average Rating**_____
(Add your ratings in this category and divide by 3)

# Self-Development Activities

## Parent Education

| | What Do You Do? | | How do you do it? | Rating |
|---|---|---|---|---|
| Do you offer any program or service to help parents deal with the challenges of child-rearing? Are any of these activities geared specifically for fathers? | | Do you make specific efforts to encourage men to attend? How do you know you are addressing the particular concerns that men have? | | |

## Support Groups

| | What Do You Do? | | How do you do it? | Rating |
|---|---|---|---|---|
| Do you provide occasions for parents to just get together to talk? Are any of these occasions set aside for fathers? Are any set aside for fathers not living at home? | | How often do you talk to men to find out if they'd like such a support program? Do you talk to the same few, or do you reach out? How many staff members are comfortable reaching out to men? | | |

## Job Training

| | What Do You Do? | | How do you do it? | Rating |
|---|---|---|---|---|
| Is there a component of your program to prepare parents for jobs? Does it include men? | | How actively do you encourage men to participate in your program? Are you aware of the shame many men feel when they don't have jobs? | | |

**Average Rating_____**

**(Add your ratings in this category and divide by 3)**

**Overall Male Involvement Profile Rating_____**

**(Add the overall average from each category and divide by 5)**

# Strategies

Now you've assessed the extent of male involvement in your program, and thought about the benefits of involving men. But just how do you do it? How do you engage fathers and others?

This section culls the strategies used by 14 model programs and others we've learned about. Some will be appropriate for your program, others won't. Some will work if you adapt them to fit your particular situation. Think of these strategies not as rules to be followed, but as ingredients for selection and modification.

We've organized these strategies into a four-stage sequence that seems to be implicit in the successful programs we've learned about. While we encourage you to pick and choose among the strategies, it's important that you understand that they follow a logical order. If you try out strategies from Stage Two and find they're not working, it may be because you haven't laid sufficient groundwork in Stage One.

### ■ Stage One: Creating a Father-Friendly Environment.

Your environment includes everything from staff attitudes to the pictures displayed in your newsletters or on your walls. It's all the elements of your program that send (or don't send) welcoming messages to your parents, whether you're aware of them or not. Remember as you go through this stage that we are defining father as any significant male in a child's life.

### ■ Stage Two: Recruiting Men to Your Program.

This refers to your specific activities to reach and include men in your program. Recruiting suggests a level of effort beyond "inviting." Many programs wonder why they are not successful at engaging men since men are always invited. The strategies presented in this section will show you just how innovative some programs have been.

### ■ Stage Three: Operating a Fathers' Program.

If and when you get men engaged, what do they do—and what do you do with them? Strategies used by other programs will give you a starting place, but this is an area where you'll be able to adapt freely, tailoring other people's ideas to fit the needs of your particular program.

### ■ Stage Four: Sustaining Male Involvement.

This refers to the difference between the activity needed to get a program started and the type of effort required to keep it going. In many ways the sustaining stage loops back to our first — creating a father-friendly environment. It takes the right soil and climate not only to start something growing, but to keep it in bloom over the long term.

**How can you help men feel comfortable in your program?**

CHAPTER

③

# Stage One: Creating a Father-Friendly Environment

Think of Stage One as the foundation for all your other efforts with fathers. But don't think of it as only benefiting men. Once you start looking at how friendly your environment is for fathers, it will force you to look at how friendly it is for mothers. If you follow the strategies offered here, you'll end up making it friendlier for both.

## Expect Men To Be Involved

As with so many things in life, you get what you expect: you won't get males involved unless you *expect* them to be involved. We convey our expectations in many ways — in what we say to parents and staff, in the notes we send (or don't send) home, even in our body language.

Here are some suggestions for getting across the message that you expect males to participate in your program:

■ **Sign Men Up Too.** Make sure your enrollment form asks for the name, address, and phone number of the father — and of any other significant male in the child's life. It's amazing how many good programs overlook this obvious step.

■ **Get Out Your Message.** Once you have dad's address, use it. Send announcements of all program events to both parents if they are not living in the same home. It's worth the postage.

*In each parent interview at the Lincoln Park Co-op Nursery in Chicago, director Judith Keller lets it be known that participation of both parents is expected and that 40 percent of the fathers participate in the classroom. Once that standard is set, newly enrolled families maintain it: that's their expectation for the program. Keller believes that when we have no expectations of fathers to participate, we get no father participation. "It's a self-fulfilling prophecy."*

*Steve Thaxton, director of the Del Paso Heights Early Childhood Center in Sacramento, California, made a point of stepping out of his office whenever he saw an especially shy dad picking up his child. In a low-key way he struck up a conversation, telling the father how happy he was to see him at the center. The next day the man lingered until Steve came out for another chat, again saying how happy he was to see him. As his trust developed, this unemployed father became a daily volunteer at the center — a place he knew he was wanted, a father-friendly place.*

■ **Say It Loud.** Make clear on all announcements that children's fathers and significant men in their lives are welcome at your program. If mom and dad are both in the home, don't just address the letter to her; address it to him too.

■ **Say It Often.** Your message about male involvement won't be convincing if you just say it at the first parent meeting. Follow through with a verbal reminder at pick-up or drop-off times; "pleasant persistence" is the name of the game.

■ **Just Ask.** Former New Dawn Head Start classroom teacher Bossie Jackson believes that often men do not participate simply because they are not asked to. "You have not because you ask not," Bossie says.

## Put Out The Welcome Mat

Men often feel "out of place" in early childhood programs. Traditionally moms interact with staff, and usually most staff are women. It's not uncommon to see a man escort his child to the playground or classroom door with a minimal amount of contact with the teachers because he does not feel comfortable in what he perceives as the "female world" of young children. An essential element in creating a father-friendly environment is to make men feel welcome. There a lot of ways for staff to make dads feel welcome:

■ **Meet and Greet Dads at the Door.** At the Cardinal Spellman Head Start center in New York City, staff members are positioned inside the lobby to greet children and parents when they enter the building. Since one of the com-

mon tasks for fathers is drop-off and pick-up, staff are always available to make contact and answer questions.

■ **Praise Children's Progress.** At the Ounce of Prevention's Garfield Daycare Center in Chicago, Illinois, the male involvement specialist, Larry Stribling, greets men at drop-off and pick-up time with a mini-progress report that always emphasizes something positive. For example: "Ming Li is learning to recognize every shape we put in front of him," or "Juanita ties her shoes without help from anyone now," or "Jahmal is so helpful at clean up time." Not a day goes by without some small positive step — even when kids are having very difficult days. So pay attention, and pass it on. You'll find dads seeking you out when they expect to hear something good about their children.

■ **Recognize Dad's Contribution.** Parents of either gender will also feel more welcome if you recognize the role they're playing in their children's lives. Just saying something like "Jose is always so happy to see you," or "Ling was singing a song about you today," will make dads feel that their presence is important. And if they feel that way, they're more likely to keep coming back.

## Find Out What Men Want

"We just don't know what men want to do!" goes the complaint. We've heard it from female staff all over the country.

Sometimes what's behind the complaint is a pair of assumptions: *men don't want* to spend time with children, or *men don't know how* to spend time with children. Either way, goes the thinking, it's not much use asking them because you won't get them to do anything. Other times, the complaint hides this assumption: *men need to be told* what they're *supposed* to want to do.

A key strategy to successful father involvement is to find out what male interests are. Don't assume that you already know. Here are some easy ways to find out, without turning yourself into a private eye or a pest:

■ **Keep Your Eyes Open.** Anytime a dad shows up at your program, or anytime a mom mentions "him," you've got a chance to learn about "his" interests. His work clothes might suggest how he spends his day. A decal on the car window might suggest he's a fan of a particular sport. His questions to (or about) his child might suggest an area of particular concern. Almost anything is possible, and you'll find out if you keep your antennae up.

■ **Ask Casual Questions.** It's amazing how much information a simple question, asked in a relaxed

*One Saturday morning workshop on male involvement concluded with the female leaders trying to plan the next event with the men. "Should we have a fishing outing, or should we go to a baseball game?" "Should we have a barbecue or go to Madison Square Garden?" What they didn't realize is that they were trying to plan the next event for the men; they were so eager to get something scheduled, to get the men to commit to a next time, that they didn't really open themselves up to what the men had to say, what they wanted to do next.*

manner, can bring forth. "So, what have you been up to lately?" or "You've sure been working hard; what's cooking?" People love it when we express genuine interest in them — even dads. Just don't press too hard or dads will feel that you're putting them on the spot, pumping for information rather than showing your concern. Again, it's the genuine interest that works.

■ **Take A Male Interest Survey.** A somewhat more formal, but also effective way of identifying interests is to distribute a mini-survey — no more than 10 or 12 questions. Ask what activities men are interested in doing — with and without their young children. Find out about their hobbies and skills. Ask what times would be convenient for them to volunteer. Keep it simple and non-threatening. A sample form is on page 26. Note that it does not ask for occupation since some men may be unemployed. However you may want to ask about current or previous occupation as that will also may be an indicator of special interests or skills. If reading or language skills are a problem, you can assign someone to ask the questions or have someone translate.

■ **Set Up A Rap Group.** Offer your fathers the space and opportunity to get together informally and to just talk. Don't set the agenda for them. The topics are for the men to choose and decide upon. Out of these meetings may come some very specific ideas about what they want to do.

## Display Images of Men

The old saying is true: "A picture *is* worth a thousand words."

The images on display at your program do more than take up space or add bright colors to your walls; they convey very important messages about its life and values.

Displaying photos or drawings that include men as well as women with young children says "men are welcome here." Moreover, you will give your preschoolers a positive image of grown-up men with children.

There are many opportunities in the life of any program to include positive images of men:

■ **Brochures.** If you have a brochure, often it's the first thing parents see about your program. It's the initial impression. And it's a good place

to start saying "men are welcome here." You can include a picture of a mom and dad together dropping off a child or chatting with a male staff member, or of a dad assisting a child with blocks or painting. The activity doesn't matter, but the underlying message does.

■ **Walls.** Make your walls speak. Hang photos of center events where men have participated. If you don't have any around, you can tear pictures of men and young children out of parenting magazines. More and more advertisements are featuring men with children; cut out the product, leave the men, and you've got your own form of advertising!

■ **Photo Contest.** A monthly contest will do wonders for your walls. One month you can ask parents to bring in the "most interesting" father and child picture they can find. Another month it can be the "funniest" or the "most artistic" or "the best picture of a grandfather and child." There's no wrong theme; the theme is just a vehicle for getting people to focus and participate. Of course, you don't have to limit the contests to images of men, vary them month-to-month to include images of women or pictures of the "whole family." And you don't have to limit participation to parents. Staff can be included or they can have their own contests, which can develop a sense of *esprit de corps*.

■ **Collages.** Collages are terrific group projects that are fun to make. Teachers, children, and parents can all bring in magazine images around a theme such as "jobs that daddies have" or "daddies and babies." Add a few jars of paste and some poster board, and you've got an afternoon activity that can go straight onto the walls.

■ **Special Occasions.** Father's Day offers a once-a-year natural opportunity to do something special to welcome men at your program. At the Cardinal Spellman Head Start Center in New York City, posters declaring "why I love my dad," are prominently displayed outside of classrooms. Jaime loved his dad because he took him to the park after school. Maria loved her dad because he bought her ice cream. Of course, many of your youngsters are physically separated from their dads and you don't want them to feel bad while other kids are "showing off." So

## TIPS

### Displaying Images of Men

• **You don't have to be an ace photographer.** The point of all this is making people feel welcome, not judged.

• **It doesn't have to cost a lot of money.** A simple point-and-shoot camera or bottom-of-the-line Polaroid will do just fine.

• **Images don't have to reflect your program in its current state.** They can give people a vision of the desired state, something you will work together to achieve in the future.

• **Do it. Don't wait around and turn this into a complicated project.** You can get it going one picture at a time, starting today.

---

*The halls and offices of the Fairfax-San Anselmo Children's Center are lined with photos of kids and families — playing, building, talking. All races naturally intermingle. So do men and women. There's no sense that the center is trying to make a statement about men and young children; but because men are so naturally a part of the pictures, they do make a statement: "This is what we expect. This is 'normal.'"*

## Male Interest Survey

**Name:** _____

**Age:** _____

**Please let us know which children you are connected to.**
**Your relationship could be as father, stepfather, uncle, brother, grandfather, friend of the mother, etc.**

| Child's Name | Child's Age | Your Relationship |
| --- | --- | --- |
| | | |

**1. Hobbies or Special Interests**

_____

_____

**2. Things I enjoy doing with my kids**

_____

_____

**3. Best time/days for me to volunteer**

_____

_____

**4. What I like to do with other men**

_____

_____

**5. What I would like to do with my child and the men's groups**

_____

_____

**6. What I would like to do with my family**

_____

_____

this activity, like any others, can be about "why I love my mom or dad."

■ **Announcements.** It's not just images or sentimental messages from kids that will make your environment more "father-friendly." Prominent postings of meetings for dads or special invitations for fathers to participate in activities will also make men feel welcome and needed.

## Recognize the Hidden Resistance from Staff

While it's likely that everybody on your staff will *think* it's a good idea to get men more involved in your program, that's not necessarily how they *feel*. And how they feel will have a lot to do with how successful you are.

How does your staff feel about getting men more involved? Their resistance may not be as overt as the examples above, but if it is predominantly female, as is typical, there are probably strong feelings — both pro and con — under the surface. Some female staff, like some of the mothers in your program, may have been abandoned or abused by men in their personal lives. It's hard not to carry those experiences into the workplace. And some are probably hesitant about yielding any women's territory to men, since men have so much territory of their own already.

Whatever the feelings and attitudes about men, unless you put them on the table in a constructive way, your program may bump into them later when you least suspect it. Here are some strategies for starting and managing a staff discussion around a topic which could be controversial:

■ **Survey Attitudes.** Our Quick Survey on Attitudes About Men and Women (right) is effective at surfacing stereotypes. Have all staff fill it out anonymously, then form small groups — separated by gender if possible — to prepare a "group summary." If there are no men on your staff, break the women up into small groups. Have one person from each group report the group summary to get the discussion going, but then open it up so that everybody participates. More important than people's answers are the stories they tell and the feelings they express in making their points.

■ **Complete the Sentence.** Have staff list as many quick responses as they can to complete the following two sentences: (1) We don't have more men involved here because... (2) We could have more men involved here if ... It's important to get responses from as many staff members as possible; don't leave out your custodial or transportation staff—they'll have ideas too.

■ **Form Discussion Groups.** If you've got a core group of men on your staff, you might separate your staff groups by gender, then bring them together to compare responses. You won't want the women's responses inhibited by men and vice versa. If you think the discussion will be most effective co-ed, try it that way.

■ **Hire a Discussion Leader.** Since the director's or head teacher's attitudes and feelings may be so important in setting the tone for the rest of your staff, it may be helpful to bring in an outside consultant to lead your discussion.

■ **Re-visit the Issue.** One discussion will probably raise more issues than it resolves. Plan to talk again after people have reflected on the subject away from the group

## Recognize the Hidden Resistance from Mothers

No matter how much mothers say about wanting to get fathers or other males involved with their children, those who have had bad experiences with men often have very mixed feelings in this area.

This ambivalence is rarely discussed, but it is very understandable. Many women have had bad experiences with their own fathers, husbands, brothers, or other men in their lives. They

> When Jimmy Jolly, head teacher at an early childhood program in Austin, Texas, tried to offer a young female colleague some advice on dealing with a difficult child, the response he got was, "I'm a woman and a mother and I know what to do." And when Stan and Ethel Seiderman of the Fairfax-San Anselmo Children's gave a workshop on "Blending the Best: Men and Women Working Together," an experienced female head teacher commented, "We've never had male staff; why would we want to?"

---

### Quick Survey

**ATTITUDES ABOUT MEN AND WOMEN**
Answer the questions with impressions drawn from your personal experience. Next to each, jot down an experience or memory that supports it.

**1. The most important contributions that fathers (mothers) can make to their kids are:**

_____

_____

**2. The greatest influence(s) on my feelings about fathers (mothers) has been:**

_____

_____

**3. I'd like the fathers (mothers) of the children in our program to:**

(a)Stop:_____

(b)Start:_____

*At the St. Bernardine's Head Start in Baltimore, a mother's group met weekly for a year before staff realized the need to set up a men's group. Again and again the women's discussion kept coming back to the anger women felt about men. Only after they felt safe talking about it among themselves could the women create a dialogue with men, which made them realize that men might need a special support group too.*

may have been abused, and fear that their children will be abused. They may have been abandoned, and fear their children will form close attachments with men and then be left wanting.

Conversely, they may fear giving up their "territory." Many, perhaps most women are still raised to feel that they are the ones primarily responsible for home and children. If they don't have work they value outside the home, then childrearing may be the backbone of their identity. To encourage men to get involved may feel like giving up a piece of that identity.

This hidden resistance from mothers is very real, very powerful, and very important for those who want to involve men. The best way to identify and begin dealing with the hidden resistance is in a series of discussion groups or workshops for mothers. Here are some guidelines for making yours work:

■ **Use an Indirect Approach.** Announcing a workshop to discuss "problems with men" might draw a crowd — but it just might scare most mothers away. While the topic is provocative and has universal appeal, it is also very threatening. It may keep mothers away, or make them feel they have to be secretive with their husbands about what they're discussing. If you announce a support group for mothers or a workshop on "common problems in motherhood," you can almost be sure that the conversation will include problems with men. If you let the topic emerge from the group, rather than force it upon them,

it is likely to be much more effective.

■ **Go Slowly.** When your group gets to the topic of men, don't rush to deal with everything at once. Very strong feelings are likely to emerge, especially from one or two people. Go slowly, and try to make sure that everybody has a chance to express their feelings and point of view. Remember a basic rule of group dynamics: no feeling that is expressed is right or wrong. We can argue with a point of view, but not with a feeling.

■ **Consider the Man's Viewpoint.** When you're in the thick of discovering mother's feelings or problems about the men in their lives, one helpful technique is to ask people to "see it from his point of view." Ask group members to say what their male friend would likely say if he were there. This can be a useful technique for building bridges in relationships or finding new ways of solving problems.

■ **Get Help from a Pro.** Strong feelings can often be frightening—to you and other group members. If you think the group you've started is too much for you to handle on an ongoing basis, you may be able to find a professional counselor or therapist to help you lead it. If you don't have a qualified person on your staff, contact one of your local social service or mental health agencies. You may even want to consider bringing in a professional right from the beginning.

■ **Get Beyond Feelings.** Identifying and acknowledging feelings is essential in dealing with mother's ambivalence about male involvement. But it's important not to let your group get stuck wallowing in feelings without any strategies for changing the situations or relationships prompting those feelings. Mothers will find it useful to share what they've done to create better relations with the men in their lives.

■ **Get Men and Women Together.** At some point, you may want to get men and women together for a dialogue. St. Bernardine's Head Start did

---

### TIPS

### Recognizing the Hidden Resistance of Mothers

• **Use the discussion starter** on this page, or adapt the Quick Survey from the preceding section.

• **Limit the number of weeks the group will meet, then extend it if necessary.** People may sign up more readily if they don't feel they have to make an ongoing commitment.

---

## Discussion Starter

Here are two surefire discussion starters for mothers' groups.

**1. My relationships with men would be better if they would:**

(a)Stop:_____

(b)Start:_____

**2. The best thing about men is:**

_____

**3. The best thing about my children's father is:**

_____

this after about six months of mothers meeting alone and it was very successful.

## Recognize the Hidden Fears of Men

It's easy to assume that men won't get involved with children because they're just not interested or don't really care as much as women do. Often, however, what shows as indifference is really a cover-up for deep-seated fears of various kinds.

In the example above, Alan's feelings may be more poignantly expressed than those of other men, but they are not atypical. Some men feel incompetent with their kids; some fear they'll be rejected; some think that women have a special natural ability with children that they'll never have. Still others may have been abandoned or rejected by their own fathers, and are acting out a repeat cycle.

It's harder to address men's hidden fears than women's for two reasons. First, if men aren't present — and are afraid to get involved — any reaching out you do may be seen as a threat. Second, if men are physically present they may be emotionally unavailable.

Much of this book is implicitly geared to addressing men's resistance. Indeed, the next two sections will show you specific ways to recruit men and ways to work with them. However, as you concentrate on creating a father-friendly environment, here are a few ideas to keep in mind:

■ **Be Aware of the Paradox.** Some men will be drawn to and others pushed away by your appeals to them as fathers. If you really want to reach all men, you'll have to recognize the difference and be prepared to use different approaches. The first group can be reached with father-child activities; the second has to be reached first with men's activities, which will lead to father-child activities.

■ **Consider the Man's Viewpoint.** A little bit of empathy can go a long way. Without turning yourself into an amateur psychologist, you can let men know that you're aware that they might be feeling insecure in your program: "It must seem strange, sometimes, coming into such a female environment; we're sure glad you're able to visit Tommy's (or Susie's) class."

■ **Empathize With Women Too.** Of course moms need empathy too, especially if they're not getting much help with the kids from the man in their life. You can let women know that you're sympathetic without taking a "let's blame the father" attitude. Indeed, you may be able to enlist his involvement through the mother: "It must be

> **A**lan, a father in his early 20's, has been coming to the Men's Group at the St. Bernardine's Head Start for almost a year. Since he and his wife separated eighteen months ago, he has hardly seen his daughter, who is now four. He is afraid he wasn't a very good father, but he misses his daughter terribly and wants to be a good father. He is turning to the group for help.

hard doing so much of this by yourself. Are there any things you think we can do to help get him more involved?" And if the man in the house does participate, you can reinforce that too.

## Create a Special Place for Men

Some men feel about as comfortable in the female-dominated environment of early childhood education as they do walking into a beauty parlor (or as many women feel walking into an auto parts store). What can you do to make the environment – both physically and psychologically – less intimidating to men? Here are some simple ideas:

■ **Rethink Your Parent Place.** If you have a space where parents can drop in and hang out, take a good look at how it's set up. If it's like most, it will have a coffee pot and a bunch of women's magazines for browsing. Try adding a few items that men may gravitate to, like *Sports Illustrated* magazine or a book like *The Father's Almanac.*

■ **Set Up a Parent Place.** If you don't have a room or special place for parents to gather, set up a spot. It may be by a bulletin board or a water cooler or in a section of the lobby where the architecture invites them to stop for a moment. Put out a table with a sign that says "parent's place" and make sure it's inviting for mothers and fathers. In addition to a coffee pot and a few magazines or books, put up special notices for moms and dads, and invite suggestions for improving your program.

■ **Set Aside a Special Time.** If you're so crowded that establishing a special place on a regular basis seems impossible, don't despair. Try scheduling a special time, once a month or once every two weeks, to utilize the special place. If you do it right, parents will look forward to it.

### TIPS

### Creating a Special Place for Men

• **Beyond creating a special physical space** for men, ask yourself "Do men feel comfortable in our program?" The psychological space you've created, the comfort zone, is just as important.

• **In your attempt to reach more men, don't accidentally slight women.** Make sure they understand you are making some special efforts so that both men and women can feel more comfortable with your program.

> **C**ardinal Spellman Head Start has set aside an entire room just for parents. It has a sofa and easy chairs, bulletin boards filled with information for parents, and a soda machine. It's simple, not frilly, and welcoming to both mothers and fathers. . . . The RAP Head Start program in St. Paul, Minnesota, makes sure to leave copies of magazines like Sports Illustrated — not just Family Circle — in its parents' area to help dads feel more comfortable.

**Every man you get involved is a potential recruiter of other men.**

CHAPTER

④

# Stage Two: Recruiting Men to Your Program

Everything you do to create a more father-friendly environment will serve your recruiting efforts. That's why it's sometimes hard to separate Stage One from Stage Two. But what sets them apart, and what you'll find here, are more specifically pro-active ways to get men involved.

### The Invisible Man in the House

Officially, four out of five Head Start families are headed by a single mother, as are many families using other child care and early education programs.

But that doesn't mean there's no man in the house. Mom's boyfriend or husband may be an active member of the family, although kept invisible so as not to jeopardize eligibility for certain benefits.

Welfare and subsidized housing or medical benefits are often tied to whether or not a man — and the income he represents — resides in the household. No man around means improved benefits.

> *The Fairfax-San Anselmo Child Care Center has a space on the admission application where the mother can identify the "significant male" in the family, even if the male is not the natural father of the child. When there is no father at home, this is a non-threatening invitation to put down the name of the grandfather, uncle, older brother, or boyfriend.*

The invisible man in the house poses a dilemma for early childhood programs in low-income communities. How do you balance the family's right to confidentiality with the need to acknowledge and include in your program a significant male in the child's life?

Here are ways to meet the "invisible man" dilemma:

■ **Intake Form.** Take a look at your intake form. Does it provide space where a "significant male" can be listed? This is an obvious place to start.

■ **Intake Interview.** After an intake form has been filled out, virtually all programs ask to meet with the parent(s) before a child is admitted. When meeting with a single mother, the parent coordinator at the Rochester Pre-K attempts to determine, as tactfully as possible, if there is a male in the household who can potentially be involved in the program. She makes it very clear that there is an official answer to the question, "Are there other adults residing in the home?" and an unofficial answer to this question. She keeps an unofficial list of males in the top drawer of her desk. The official male resident of the household or the unofficial male is targeted for possible involvement in the program.

■ **All-Staff Alert.** At Rochester Pre-K and the Cardinal Spellman program on the lower east side of New York City, program directors have sensitized the entire staff to be alert—without being nosy—for the presence of a male in the life of the child. All staff are required to "hang out" in the corridors, lobby, and parent rooms before and after classes. They are looking for the men who bring children to school or drop off mother and child in front of the center in their car, so that they can begin creating informal relationships.

■ **Trusting Relationships.** Jacqueline Garner, parent liaison at St. Bernardine's Head Start in Baltimore, operates with the assumption that "most people are not going to tell you there's a man in the home until they feel comfortable with you." She waits until she has built a relationship with the parent, then "somewhere after a child has been in the program they may tell you, 'this is so-and-so's father' or, 'my friend.' — that's how you find out about that connection."

■ **Surveys.** Twice a year the Men's Group in the Rochester Pre-K program sends out a short questionnaire to men that are not involved whom the women in the program suggested contacting. The survey has a dual purpose. It advertises the existence of the Men's Group and it helps identify the significant males in the children's lives. Since the survey is being conducted by the parents, rather than the staff, it seems to be less threatening to the other parents.

## Bus Drivers As Recruiters

If your program provides transportation, your bus or van drivers – because of their frequent contact with parents – are an important force for recruiting men into your program.

Often the driver has more daily contact with parents than anybody else on the staff, including the parent coordinator. The driver is likely to see a child's parents at either the beginning or end of the day. If a child needs medication, the driver has to receive it and make sure instructions are communicated clearly to other program staff. If a message needs to be sent back home, it's often the driver's job to relay it.

While drivers can be male or female, in many programs the largest percentage of male staff is in the transportation (or janitorial) pool. And they may be more ready and able than you've ever thought to help get other men involved.

Here are some ways to tap the power of your transportation staff as a recruiting force:

■ **Recruit Volunteer Riders.** In some Head Start programs it's mandatory to have volunteer riders on the bus, so that the driver won't be alone with twenty preschoolers. At Parents in Community Action (PICA), which serves 2,000 families in Hennepin County, Minnesota, the 54 drivers take responsibility for getting that support. When Michael Griffen pulls up and sees a father standing at the bus stop he says, "Yo dude! You ride the bus tomorrow!" He even knocks on the doors to see if there's a man in the house who can ride the bus. "This is one way to begin getting men involved," says PICA's

## The Invisible Man in the House

• **Make your policies on confidentiality very clear to parents.** They should know what information must be collected and reported to funding agencies, governmental sources, etc., and what information does not have to be reported. Parents should understand the rules of the game.

• **Be sure you understand the government policies that apply to your program.** Public assistance policies are often quite complicated and there is a lot of mythology that surrounds these policies. In Dallas, Texas for example, there is a local welfare policy that rewards rather than penalizes. Mothers and fathers of children receive extra monthly cash benefits if the father formally declares that he is the father of the child.

*At the Whitfield Parent-Child Center in Dalton, Georgia, Neil Swinney has the combined title of Bus Driver/Father Coordinator. Every day Neil's old yellow school bus travels the dirt roads of this poor rural community to pick up or drop off children. But once a week he makes a special trip, riding out to find "the man of the house," who may be a father or a live-in boyfriend. "They're so used to seeing this bus that it's not threatening," says Neil. "I drive up and invite myself in for a cup of coffee or a chat on the porch. We talk about anything — the weather, the economy. I just try to get to know them. That's the beginning of getting them involved."*

## TIPS

### Bus Drivers As Recruiters

• **Don't make drivers second-class citizens.** They have a different job, but an important job. Make sure the rest of your staff knows that.

• **Include them in your staff meetings.** Even if they are not at all meetings, it's important for the staff to see them as part of the whole team.

• **Ask them what they've observed.** They may know a lot more than you realize about what's going on with kids and their families.

• **Expand their hours.** Even if you can't afford to hire transportation staff full-time, get them into the classroom on a regular basis.

Bryan Nelson. "Once they get to know the kids on the bus, they're much more likely to volunteer."

■ **Turn Riders into Classroom Volunteers.** Riding the bus can be just a first step to fuller involvement. After children are dropped off at PICA, for example, there's often a half-hour to an hour before the bus driver takes the parent volunteer back home. "That's time for parents to see the program in action," says Nelson, "and it's an opportunity for them to be in their child's classroom. Soon they're really hooked on the program." So hooked that PICA has created a Parent Training Program, a six-week series that combines work in the classroom with instruction about child development. One father who started as a volunteer rider is now a full-time staff member at the center!

■ **Turn Drivers Into Classroom Volunteers.** In the PACE program in Hattiesburg, Mississippi, the situation was reversed. The male bus driver became one of the program's most dedicated volunteers in the classroom because he saw one of the fathers doing it.

■ **Recognize Drivers as a Resource.** Rick, the van driver for the Addison County Parent-Child Center covers over 150 miles each day picking up clients in this rural section of Vermont. The long van rides full of casual conversation put him in an important position to learn about both parents and children, and about ways to improve the center's services. Because of his direct association with the men and women of this teen parent center, Rick is a regular attendee at the center's staff meetings.

■ **Hire from the Community.** Johnny Sanchez, the van driver with the Avance parent education program in San Antonio, Texas, used to be one of its clients. Because he's from the community that the program serves, he garnered immediate trust—and has become an important source of information about families and outreach to men. "If I know one of the men is having a problem, I tell Isaac, the director, about it," says Johnny.

At Chicago's *Ounce of Prevention*, Larry Stribling is paid to get men involved. Larry is one of three part-time staff members with the title of "male involvement specialist." These men actively encourage fathers and other significant males to act as chaperones on class outings, attend special dad's meetings, or volunteer in the classroom. One of the specialists is a Head Start father himself. The second is a Head Start uncle. The third doesn't have a Head Start child in the program. But all three men were recruited from the community that the program serves.

■ **Redefine the Role.** To fully tap the talent of its drivers, the PICA program has redefined their role, making them an integral part of each classroom's teaching team. Drivers now work 40 hours instead of 30, are required to spend part of every day in the classroom, and are full participants at all teacher meetings and parent-teacher meetings. They are respected for their knowledge of how children behave on the bus, and they are expected to observe children in the classroom as well, and contribute their insights to the rest of the team.

### Paid Staff As Recruiters

There is no one right way to go about recruiting more men into your program. But, it sure helps if you have the financial resources to hire someone to do it.

Even if you can't afford to hire a specialist, you can enlist the staff you are already paying to help get men involved. A lot depends not on your budget, but on your attitude about what you expect your staff to accomplish.

■ **Enlist Social-Service Staff.** At the Miami Valley Child Development Center in Ohio, social service staff take it seriously that their job is to work with the whole family. As they travel from center to center working with families, they are always trying to establish a relationship with a man in the house and encourage his participation.

■ **Find a Male Champion.** One person with commitment can be the spark for the whole team. At the PICA Head Start in Minneapolis, Bryan Nelson's official title is Coordinator of Health Services. But because he's so committed to getting men more involved in early education, his presence is a continual consciousness raiser for the whole staff. He keeps them ever-vigilant about ways to encourage more men to be involved. Jordan Engel plays the same role at the Addison County Head Start in Vermont.

■ **Find a Female Champion.** Your champion doesn't have to be a male of the species. In Rochester, New York, the women in charge of the Florence S. Brown Pre-K program took the initiative to get a father's group going, then stood back and let it develop. In Hattiesberg, Mississippi, the female leaders of the PACE program took on the cause of recruiting men from the community.

■ **Set the Tone You Want.** Staff aren't likely to reach out to fathers unless the director has made it clear that's something the program values. At the Fairfax-San Anselmo Children's

Center in California, director Ethel Seiderman has conveyed clearly that fathers and other men are important in children's lives, as does Joanne Milano at the Cardinal Spellman Head Start in New York City.

By the way, maybe you **can** afford a male involvement specialist. Find a champion on your staff and give him or her the extra title of "male involvement specialist." The recognition that comes with a new title may be reward enough to get things going.

## Men as Recruiters

Every man you get involved — by whatever means — is a potential recruiter of other men. Men can reach out to other men in many different ways. Here are just a few:

■ **Who Do You Know?** It's usually easier to approach somebody you already know — or somebody who knows somebody you know — rather than a total stranger. Have your already-committed men review your list of parents. Who knows whom? What do they know about him — or her? What would be the best way to make contact? Remember, it doesn't have to be just guys calling guys; if somebody knows the woman in the house, she can be contacted to lead you to the man of the house.

■ **One on One.** Every guy who has played basketball is familiar with the one-on-one defense. You can make recruitment something of a game by turning it into the one-on-one offense. Assign a potential recruit to one of your already-committed members. The member's job is to find a way to engage the targeted recruit in your program, using any tactics he can create. Of course you can give suggestions about how to recruit, but you can also leave it up to the imagination of your members to figure out the strategy.

■ **Pound the Pavement.** To recruit men in Minneapolis for the fledgling "Dad and Me," Bob Broncali and Ron Gustafson adopted the approach of political canvassers. They put on their good walking shoes and beat the pavement, going door-to-door to drum up interest. It was a lot of work, but by doing it together they were able to share and soften the pain of rejection. And they were able to celebrate their shared accomplishment — recruits. A small nucleus of men today have "Dad and Me" groups going throughout the city.

■ **Find a Partner.** Is there a college or university in your area that needs to find fieldwork experience for advanced students? The Philadelphia Parent-Child Center teamed up with Temple

*At the Florence S. Brown Pre-K program in Rochester, members of the men's group do most of the recruiting — with a little help from the parent group leader and other staff. As Gerald Daniels says, "When we see a father bringing his child to school, we always find a way of talking to him. Sometimes we put a little pressure on; besides just saying 'Hi,' we give additional information about the father's group. It's sometimes effective in making them show up."*

University to allow a social work student/star football player to fulfill some of his requirements as a facilitator of a men's group. The center gains, the men gain, and the student even gets college credit for his work.

■ **Share Your Strategies.** You'll learn a lot in your attempts to reach other men, and what you learn will be different from the next person. It's important to share what you're learning as you go. It will be confirming and it will give you new ideas to try out.

## Women as Recruiters

Male involvement often starts with female involvement. A man will often get involved if there is an active interest on the part of the child's mother or a female staff member. Here are a few ways that women can help men get involved in programs for young children:

■ **Encourage Mothers to Encourage Men.** "We start at home," says one staff member at Parent's as Teachers in Missouri. "We encourage the wife to encourage the husband or other significant male to come. It takes us to encourage them." And sometimes it produces big results and gratitude. According to one dad at the Florence S. Brown Pre-K program in Rochester, "I wouldn't be here if my wife hadn't encouraged me to be here."

■ **Be Patient and Persistent.** Just because you're encouraging doesn't mean he'll jump right in there. "I would love to have my husband involved and I think he'll learn about how to understand our son better if he comes to the Head Start program," says Peggy, a member of the parent policy council in the Miami Valley

### TIPS

### Men As Recruiters

• **When you are recruiting, you are in the business of building relationships.** Your goal should be not just to recruit, but to make every person you speak to feel good about your program and about you. If you begin to establish a relationship, then you've laid the foundation for a later approach, which might not be until next year.

• **Don't push too hard or fast.** While it's important to encourage and coax people, you also don't want to turn them off.

*After almost 14 years of providing parent education for women, Avance of San Antonio, Texas, started teaching men with the same curriculum; they did so because men were seeing the gains that women were making. Soon they learned that it needed to be adapted and amended so that it could be directed to concerns expressed by men. Still, it was the women who led the way for the men, and led the men into the program.*

**A man will often get involved if there is an active interest on the part of the child's mother or a female staff member.**

Child Development Centers in Ohio. "I just keep pushing. One day, I know he'll come to a meeting." Programs that have been successful at involving men recognize woman's strong influence in this area.

■ **Encourage Women to Show Their Enthusiasm.** A mother's enthusiasm can rub off on her male partner. At the Texas Migrant Council Head Start, men used to wait outside in their trucks while women attended parent advisory meetings. But curiosity got the better of them when they saw how interested the women were. Slowly they started attending meetings and soon they were hooked.

■ **Work With Women on Involving Their "Ex-es."** Sometimes providing services to women can lead them to invite men in. In women's groups at the St. Bernardine's Head Start in Baltimore, Parent Liaison Jacqueline Garner had been surfacing and dealing with a lot of anger towards men. With the support of her colleague, Clarence Tucker, she began asking the mothers some provocative questions: "Do you feel your children need their father? Can he take the children for a day? Can you let go of your anger for a little bit so the father can have a relationship with the children?" The ensuing discussion led some of the mothers to invite their ex- or estranged husbands to a male-female relationship group meeting to begin pursuing answers. It was the first step in hooking the fathers back into the children's lives

■ **Jump In – Then Step Back.** At the Rochester Pre-K program, director Jan Scura teamed up with Janet McElrath, parent coordinator, to get more men involved. But they recognized early

on that they would have to step out of the way and let the men take charge as quickly as possible. They attended some of the early meetings, suggested agenda items, and then spent the rest of their time developing the leadership potential of the group. The men's group now has its own male leaders. Jane and Janet don't attend the group meetings any more. They don't have to. It is self-sustaining, but the communication between the men's program and the program administration are excellent.

■ **Enlist Moms As Marketers.** In Minnesota, there is a very active marketing effort underway—by moms. They actively promote the program at home and many even sign their husbands up for the weekly father-child sessions. They attribute much of their success to the word-of-mouth advertising created by the women and their direct efforts to involve their men. The program has had 600 children from 450 families go through the program in two years. The 45 dads who came were there because the women promoted the program.

## Reach Out To the Hard-to-Reach

Some fathers seem impossible to reach. They never show up at the center. They never show any interest in their children.

Some of these "abandoning" fathers are men with very low self-esteem, ashamed if they are unemployed and ashamed that they have been "bad" fathers. They don't know how to connect with their kids, or they won't risk trying because they fear yet another failure in their lives. To reach these men you may need to take some special steps.

Men don't have to be in prison to be among the hard-to-reach. They may have moved away or they may even live down the block. Here are approaches that worked for some programs to

*In Sampson County, North Carolina, they don't assume that an imprisoned father is a father who doesn't want to be involved with his children. They have started a "Writing to Dad" program and the dads and their kids love it. With the help of her teacher, Yvonne writes to her father, who is incarcerated in a nearby prison. Yvonne loves it when Dad writes back. They may be separated but the letters they share keep them together.*

reach these men and make them part of children's lives:

■ **Indirect Approach.** St. Bernardine's Head Start in Baltimore, Maryland reaches fathers through the weekly meeting of its "Men's Group." Interestingly, none of the fathers who attended at first were fathers of Head Start children. But that didn't bother group leader Clarence Tucker: "We know we are reaching the fathers because the fathers hang on the same street corners with the men who are showing up. We know that the word is starting to spread about the importance of staying connected with their kids. We're starting to get to the fathers in our program, but by a different route."

■ **Double Mailings.** How do you reach the father who isn't living at home? The Pre-K center in Rochester, New York reaches him by sending literature from the center to both addresses. Duplicate copies of information about meetings, a progress report, and information about programs are sent to the home of the child and to the address where the father is known to live. When parents are divorced, it is never assumed that information sent to one will get to the other. "Unless you do it this way, you never know," says the program supervisor.

■ **Including Fathers in the Home Visit.** Family workers in the Parents as Teachers program in St. Louis, Missouri, make home visits as part of the program and provide parent training to whomever is in the home at the time. But what if the father or other significant male isn't there? This doesn't stop them from at least making a contact. They leave notes such as "Sorry you couldn't be with us today. Today we worked on ......" The message is clear. "We missed you. You're important in this!" Of course, they do as much as they can to schedule home visits when the father is going to be home.

## Reaching Out to All Men

You don't have to limit your outreach to fathers — or even to another man in the household or family. Your community includes lots of men who can serve as role models or father figures for children in your program.

■ **Local Businessmen.** In an approach that is similar to the one used in Hattiesburg, Betty Toney of the Miami Valley Child Development Center, a Head Start program in Dayton, Ohio, started "Manpower". Betty sent out flyers to area churches and businesses inviting men to come visit children in the classroom to

tell stories, tell about their work—anything as long as they could be there to be positive role models for the children.

■ **High School Students.** Cardinal Spellman Head Start in New York City has an on-going relationship with a local high school. Young men (and women) serve full time, full day, unpaid internships in Head Start classrooms. Both the young men and the boys and girls in the classroom gain from this experience. As Marty, a 17 year old says, "Many of the children don't have male figures in their home. They need to have adults around who have time to spend with them. Sometimes one of the children will run up to me and ask me to read a story, just like that. Kids need adults around who can do this."

■ **Volunteers.** In Dallas, Bobbie Thresh, an employee of Texas Instruments, has been convincing men who are parents or friends of students in the Dexter Elementary School to volunteer in the classroom for ten years. Not everyone

> The PACE Head Start in Hattiesburg, Mississippi reached out to John Tatum, CEO of Willmut Gas Company, a major employer in the area, to help start the "Male Role Model Program." Now they have twenty men from local churches, businesses, and the local U.S. Army base who volunteer in classrooms as teacher assistants, serve lunch, and escort children on field trips.

**Reaching the Hard to Reach**

• **It may seem obvious, but make sure you schedule program meetings at times that make it possible for both the male and female in the house to attend.** Some programs even have two meetings on a particular day to accommodate different parent schedules.

**Your community includes lots of men, not just family members, who can serve as role models or father figures.**

**It is ultimately the experience men have with children that will keep them coming back.**

them for the long haul. The program that you provide for them ultimately will be the thing that keeps them coming back.

There are many different ways of providing extrinsic rewards for male involvement if you decide that this is important to your program. Here are some examples:

■ **Lucky Bucks.** Cardinal Spellman, a Head Start center on the lower east side of New York City, provides tangible rewards for parents who volunteer their time through a program they have labeled "Lucky Bucks." Local businesses donate goods to the program: a small shopping cart, table fans, and trays from a hardware store; a turkey and gift certificates for a sandwich and a coke from a local delicatessen; shoes from a shoe store. When parents donate in-kind services, they accumulate "Lucky Bucks" — paper vouchers that can be traded for some of the gifts in the center's "store." Director Joanne Milano thinks that Lucky Bucks are not the only reason that parents volunteer but "It helps. It's a little something."

■ **Reimbursement.** Parents, both men and women in the program in Dayton, Ohio, receive $10 for each literacy class they attend. The money is paid at the completion of each session and is considered to be reimbursement for travel, babysitting, etc.

■ **Recognition.** Broaden your view of tangible inducements to include recognition of parent involvement with "thank you" notes, letters from the children telling daddy, grandpa, uncle or friend how much they like having him come to the center. Putting pictures of daddy and child on the center's walls also become tangible rewards for male involvement.

who comes to the weekly men's group or to volunteer in the classroom is a parent of a child in the school, but they come anyway. Many enjoy simply getting together with other men from the community.

■ **Adopt-a-Program.** In Houston, Texas, high school classes have "adopted" Head Start classes. Boys visit, bring pictures of themselves in uniforms, play sports with the children and act as chaperones on field trips. Everyone benefits.

■ **Cast A Wide Net.** There's no limit to the groups in your community who may want to form partnerships with you and who would be willing to send men who'll get involved with your program. Some likely candidates are: Kiwanis or other men's service organizations; churches and synagogues which often have a "brotherhood" or men's group that meets regularly; and groups such as doctors, lawyers, accountants, etc. that have local professional associations. Get started with a directory of organizations from your local Chamber of Commerce. Don't forget public employees including firefighters, police officers, school teachers, and coaches!

## Make Dollars Talk

Men should be more involved with young children because of the intrinsic joys, right? That should be inducement enough. But what about some small extrinsic rewards to encourage involvement? Are they appropriate? Do they work? Opinions differ, but if you feel you should, consider the inducement as a way of getting parents attention, not as a way of keeping

*S*ue Harding and Cheryl Mitchell of the Addison County Parent/Child Center in Vermont, designed to help low income teenagers become better parents, think dollars talk. Fathers (and mothers) in the program get $1.00 an hour for working in child care, taking classes, and working in the center's car detailing and packaging businesses. According to Sue and Cheryl this relatively small amount of money is a significant motivator for involvement and is eagerly sought after by the moms and dads.

## CHAPTER

## 5

# Stage Three: Operating a Fathers' Program

**As men learn to trust your program they will feel more comfortable talking about fatherhood.**

You may have a desire to rush ahead with educational programming about being a father. That may suit some men, but not others.

One of the objectives of Stage Two, Recruiting, was to find out about men's needs and interests and build on them. The same goes for Stage Three, Operating a Fathers' Program. Men have to feel comfortable before they will become active, regular participants in your program. So a good many of the strategies we'll offer you here have to do with dispelling men's anxieties or feelings of inadequacy as fathers and helping them feel comfortable getting together.

### For-Men-Only Events

One of the best ways to get men more involved with their children and your program is to not ask them to get more involved with their children and your program.

The explanation for that puzzling contradiction is actually quite simple. Before they can take care of their children's needs, all parents need to feel that someone is helping take care of their needs. One of those needs is to feel included in a group, to connect with others.

So, one of the best ways to get men hooked into your program is by helping them to connect with other men in "manly" ways. Once they have other guys to relate to in your program they may feel more comfortable about participating with children.

*The Parent-Child Center in Oakland, California holds a "Car Wash for Dads" four times a year. The center provides buckets, soap, hoses and rags, and everybody has a good time washing cars. "After there's a social linkage we try to get them involved in the agenda of the center," says director Gary Thompson.*

## For-Men-Only Events

• **Find out what dads do to "get away from it all."** Make this a planned activity with your program as sponsor.

• **Don't assume you know what dads are interested in.** Some groups may love going to an NBA game, others might prefer a camping trip. Do your best to assess what would be universally interesting to the men in your program.

• **Keep at it.** One event usually isn't enough for friendships to flourish.

• **Don't be surprised if some of the women in your program resent the fact that you've planned something special for the men, and not them.** This is a potentially serious source of division. Be sure that your program is equitable, providing events for both men and women.

There is no end to the types of social events you can create to bring fathers and other significant males together. We've come across bowling, fishing, bleacher seats at baseball games, football evenings and even a dad's only gambling trip to Reno. Here are some specific examples:

■ **Fishing for Catfish (and Men).** At the Whitfield Parent-Child Center in Dalton, Georgia, bus-driver and father's group coordinator Neil Spinney rambles out to visit men who are in the home and invites them to go bowling or fishing—as bait. "A lot of these guys don't have any extra money to do anything extra for themselves." The social activity is strictly for them and strictly for fun. The fishery at the University of Georgia is in the same county as the center. Dads can go there and fish for catfish and pay by the pound. One guy, according to Neil, caught a ten pounder. "It was a record for the area, and it nearly broke us!" Eventually, dads end up volunteering to be part of the program's activities that put them together with their children. But the first social activities are strictly for men only.

■ **Playing Ball.** If you've got access to a basketball court or playing field, you may have just what you need to get a group of guys together. In Minneapolis, Minnesota, social worker Eric Ziegler doesn't invite men to join the fathers' groups he runs. Instead, he invites them to shoot a few hoops at the elementary school gym. After the men are comfortable with each other, and comfortable knowing that Eric is a "regular guy," they become interested in participating in more father-oriented activities. A good game of softball or touch football has the same effect.

■ **Watching a Ball Game.** Some guys are into playing, others into watching. If they have limited incomes, many will have never attended a professional sporting event. So it can be quite a special occasion if you can get a block of tickets, even if they are high up. That sort of event can make a lasting impression and breed lots of loyalty to your program. And if you can't afford tickets, try a Monday night football gathering in front of the television; one program in Washington state tried this with great success.

■ **Meeting the "Fighting Irish".** The South Bend, Indiana Head Start program has used its proximity to the Notre Dame campus to good advantage. On Males Night Out the men of Head Start get to meet prominent sports figures from the legendary sports powerhouse. There are door prizes, light refreshments, autographs, and a picture session. Autographed basketballs and footballs are given out. According to family service advocate Cannie Phillips, "It was an idea that really worked for us." Granted, there is only one Notre Dame, but your local college or university might still provide enough of a draw to get guys out.

■ **Meeting the Coach.** Bob Brancale had a similar idea for enlisting male interest in the Early Childhood Family Education program in Minneapolis, where hockey is a local passion. Brancale arranged for the Northstars' coach to be available on a Saturday morning. The coach didn't push the early childhood program, but he did talk about his own father—how much that relationship meant to him. It made the point, and lots of men later signed up for the program.

### Men's Work, Men's Play

For many men, the most comfortable way to get involved is through activities that they think of as "men's work"—fixing things. Since there's no end to the fixing-up that needs to be done at most programs, there are many ways to use this approach to get men involved. But here are a few categories to help you think about soliciting male involvement:

■ **Large-Group Projects.** Invite men to help out with fix-up or clean-up days. Emphasize the fact that you really need their brawn — and brains — to get things in shape and that a concentrated effort by as many men as can help will do wonders. One year after instituting a One-Saturday-a-Month fix-up day, a center in Chicago has 27 men volunteering on a regular basis.

■ **Playground Projects.** It's hard to resist the call to create or repair a playground for kids. Nobody has to be an expert, and everybody can see the tangible rewards when kids use the new tire swing or play in the new sand box.

■ **Small-Team Projects.** Because they've grown up with sports — watching, playing, or being told they should be playing — most men are comfortable with being on (and competing on) a team. Invite men to sign up for different "teams" and assign a captain or team leader to each. One can be the bike repair team, another the playground team, and so forth. Men will

---

*The WCIC Playmate Child Development Center in Sacramento, California gets men involved by "giving the male something concrete and positive" to do at the center. Alpha Bruton, policy council chairperson, says that the males in her program like coming around to keep up the building. They hang pictures, repair playground equipment and fix broken toys.*

like the camaraderie, and they'll enjoy the friendly competition with other teams if you make it known how well each team is doing.

■ **Individual Projects.** Some guys don't like groups or teams, or their schedules won't allow them to participate when everyone else is. Try to find out about any particular interest or skill a man may have, and then make room for an individual project. That might mean coming in once a week — or once a month — to check the bicycles, fix the gutters, or whatever.

■ **Hard Jobs.** Often there is a particularly hard job that nobody at the center wants to do. At the Fairfax-San Anselmo Children's Center, that's replacing lightbulbs in 25-foot-high ceilings, which requires standing on top of a 10-foot ladder and reaching up with a 10-foot pole with an unscrewing mechanism on the end. Who can you call? The monthly men's group! After they have breakfast, they go from room to room changing bulbs. That is, six guys who are scared of heights stand around like a human safety net while one brave soul climbs the ladder.

■ **Special Skills.** It's not just with mechanical fix-up skills that men can lend a hand. Any special skill they have and feel comfortable providing will do. At one program in New York City, a man who works as a barber volunteers whenever he can to give the children free haircuts (with prior parental approval!)

■ **Odd Jobs.** Every program has a few jobs that need to be done every once in a while, like buying new food for the guinea pigs or hauling cartons of paper towels from the local discount store. Perfect to pitch to one of your men!

■ **Kitchen Patrol.** Does preparing and serving food put a strain on your staff? In a housing project in Dallas, one program recruits men to help out with mealtime, then gives them a free lunch. As the men get to know the program and the children, they may volunteer in other ways.

■ **Work and Eat.** Even if they're not doing kitchen patrol, a nice incentive and reward for guys is to offer them a meal or snack either before or after they work for you. For an all-day-Saturday clean-up, for example, some programs will start with a breakfast, others will end with a dinner, and still others will provide munchies all day long.

## Ice Breakers

Once you've been successful in gathering a group of men together to form a rap group, a father's group, a dad's club, or whatever you (or they) have decided to call it, you will immediate-

> *D*arryl Reeves, family advocate for the Camden Head Start program, unwraps a roll of toilet paper in front of the group, then passes it around the room. Each man is instructed to tear off a section — not just one sheet, but a section. Darryl never says how much to tear off, or how it will be used, but as the roll makes its way around the room, the laughter and joking get louder and louder.

ly be confronted with a need to "break the ice." All groups that are first forming require a little warming up to overcome the anxiety that comes with the initial meeting of people who don't know one another too well.

Here are some sample ice-breaking techniques that have been used by others to get things rolling:

■ **Toilet-Paper Talk.** Darryl Reeves could probably break the ice just by passing the toilet paper around, but he doesn't stop there. After everybody has a piece, Darryl gives these instructions: "We will now go around the room again. For every sheet of toilet paper that you tore off, you have to tell us something about yourself, something that defines who you are." At this point participants tend to hold up what they've torn off and let it dangle down; it's pretty clear who took three sheets and who took thirty! And he who took thirty has a lot to say about himself.

■ **People Bingo.** In White Bear Lake, Minnesota, parent educator Lowell Johnson likes to start the first meeting of the Dad and Me men's group with "People Bingo." He hands out cards that look exactly like bingo cards with one difference (see page 40). Instead of displaying numbers, the boxes on each card contain different descriptive phrases such as "likes ice fishing," "sings in the shower," "big Twins fan," etc. The object of the card is to fill a row, column, or diagonal with the name of a person in the group who fits that particular description.

The structure of the game literally forces participants to talk to as many other men as they can. With the timer set for ten or fifteen minutes, a lot of very personal—and very funny—questions get asked. The cards are all different. When each man's bingo card is filled, he gets to choose one box and introduce the man who matches it, adding whatever else he has learned about that man during their brief introduction to one another. As men are introduced, others cross out boxes, until everyone has been introduced. The activity is fun, leads to lots of laughter, and the bingo cards are easy to make.

As you glance at the bingo card, you can see that it could be amended to make it more serious, with the boxes relating to some aspect of

## TIPS

### Men's Work and Play

• **Men don't have to be experts to get involved.** One can learn from another. So you can pitch the bike-repair day as a chance to come learn how to repair a bike.

• **Advertise the "work" you need help with** as a great way to meet some buddies.

• **Acknowledge the work men have done** — in your signs, in your newsletter, at your parent meetings. That will get more men coming next time.

• **Don't leave women out.** There's no reason why women can't fix things, and it's important not to let your recruiting be taken as a sign of excluding or discriminating against women.

| People Bingo | | | | |
|---|---|---|---|---|
| Drinks mineral water | Has 3 children | Creative | In danger of shopping addiction | Ethnic traditions important |
| Twins in extended family | Dislikes most sports | Wears socks with holes | Football fan | Cream cheese lover |
| Has kids in elementary | Is pregnant | FREE | Needs coffee | Has made lifestyle changes |
| Does needlework | Occasionally disagrees with spouse | Needs more recipes | Politically active | Is physical |
| Feels positive about laundry | Has mood swings | Chocolate is important in life | Goes north regularly | Wants more children |

child rearing: "thinks spanking a child is appropriate," "doesn't believe in spanking," "feels uneasy about holding an infant," "feels comfortable holding an infant," etc. This game can be used again and again, throughout the year, whenever you want to broach a new topic with the group. It's a good way to get a discussion going around a sensitive topic.

■ **Positive Speaking.** It's usually pretty easy to get people to say something positive about parenting. You can have people introduce themselves by saying their name and "the one thing you like most about being a parent," or "the thing your children like most about you as a parent" or "the best experience you've had with your kids." After they've started with the positive, you can ask them to talk about some of the stresses and strains of parenthood: Tell us "the hardest thing about being a parent."

Men can share this information with each other, first in pairs, then in small groups, then in the large group. Obviously, this technique lends itself to all sorts of questions to get things rolling, such as "How were you parented?" or "How are you parenting now?"

■ **Pairs of Strangers.** A standard ice breaker that can be used successfully in almost any setting is simply asking men to pair off with someone they don't know and introduce themselves. Then each person has to introduce the other person to the larger group. You can prompt the introductions with serious or silly questions, written on a blackboard, on three by five cards, etc.

■ **Baseball-Card Dads.** At the Minneapolis Early Childhood Family Education program, Bob Brancale helps break the ice by having each man create a baseball card about himself as a dad. Each card should contain a man's name, nick-

name, and major and minor league parenting experiences. To make this more realistic, men can be asked to bring a picture of themselves to the first meeting or, if you have the equipment, you can take polaroid photos on the spot for this purpose. Men learn a lot about one another in trying to fill the cards out and reading them to the group or passing them around when they are completed.

■ **Personal Want Ad.** Make believe you have to be gone from your family for a while and have to write an ad for a replacement for yourself. Lowell Johnson does this and has men read their want ads aloud, providing lots of laughs—a real ice breaker!

■ **The Shoe Game.** Lowell Johnson also plays the Shoe Game with new dads. Everyone takes off one shoe and throws it to the leader. The leader throws any shoe to one person in the circle, who then throws it to someone else. The first time around it's a good idea to have everyone raise his hand after he's caught and thrown a shoe. The purpose is to create a pattern of catching and throwing that is consistent—everyone catches from the same person and throws to the same person every time. The leader is the first to throw each shoe and the first one in the circle to catch it. Once the pattern has been established, the leader proceeds to throw out the shoes one after another until they have all traversed the entire circle and come back. Soon the air is filled with flying and colliding shoes and the group is having great fun.

■ **Zoom Pa.** Lowell Johnson also likes to use the Zoom Pa warm-up. Everyone stands in a circle and selects one person to be "it." "It" says "zoom" if he wants to pass "it" to the person on his left, or "pa" if he wants to pass "it" to the right. The new person who is "it" then says "zoom" or "pa" to pass "it" along. This game moves fast and sometimes develops into a battle of wills if two people keep passing "it" back to each other. If this happens (and if this is a problem), the leader can introduce a third command, "finigliaro." Finigliaro allows "it" to pass "it" across the circle by pointing at someone as he says the command. The game creates lots of laughs.

■ **Safari.** Ask people to pick the animal they'd most like to be if they could be an animal. Or have them pick the animal they are most like. Then go around the room and have people say their name, their animal, and why they picked that animal. You can learn a lot about people very quickly this way.

■ **Country of Origin.** Bob Brancale keeps a map of the world in the room where the men are meeting. He asks men to place pins in the country or countries of their origin. Then he asks each man to talk about how their roots have affected their parenting.

All of these ice breakers help overcome the stiffness that sometimes comes with a group encounter. While many provoke laughter, they can open the door for serious discussions later on. They also send a message to men that they will find support and friendliness in this place, and that the learning about their children that is to come may be fun. You'll notice also that most of the games are non-competitive in nature, again because men are looking for support, not to be tested.

## Men's Groups

Men are often drawn to a place where they can talk to other men in a supportive atmosphere. And they don't have to go off to the woods for a "wild man" retreat to do it!

A number of programs have developed successful "rap" or discussion groups for men. Some of the talk may turn to fatherhood, but it doesn't have to. As they build alliances with one another, as they learn to trust your program as a place that cares for them—as well as for mothers and children — they will feel more comfortable talking about fatherhood.

Here are some different approaches that may work for you:

■ **Use Food as an Incentive.** The monthly meeting of the Men's Group at the St. Bernardine's Head Start in Baltimore nourishes both body and soul. A rap group starts at 6 p.m. with men dropping in anytime during the next half hour or so. At 7:30 discussion continues, but over a meal prepared by the center's cook. Mealtime is a chance for men to talk one-on-one or in small clusters about the issues they've been dealing with during the previous hour or so. For men living in poverty, mealtime may be the item that draws them to the program in the first place. However, it's a good idea to have food on hand for any group.

■ **Use Staff as Group Leaders.** At the Addison County Child Development program, young men meet at least twice a week for an hour. One session is led by the staff co-directors, who set the agenda around topics such as job preparation, conflict resolution in families, and planning for recreation. The second session is led by two social workers, with the discussion directed more towards life skills and personal adjustment matters.

■ **Offer a Mentor.** Boston men who are members of THE CLUB meet once a week in a group with their mentors, who are professional men with standing in the community. Discussions in these three-hour meetings cover a broad range of topics: resume writing, substance abuse, civil rights, job preparation, etc. Some meetings are set aside for individual member's concerns. On "Open Forum" night the floor is open to any topic that is brought up by a particular member. On one evening the group discussed the concerns of one member who feared he might be losing his job. The rules are simple—just let them feel comfortable talking to one another— but the effects can be profound.

■ **Use the First Ten Minutes Well.** The first ten minutes are critical to the comfort level of your group and the flow of your discussion. At the Merrywood School's program for fathers of children with disabilities, James May places great importance on introductions. "We use enormous name tags," he says. "When a new guy walks in, another guy gives him a name tag, takes him on a tour, and introduces him to the other guys."

■ **Let Everyone Take Some Responsibility.** There are usually seven or eight things that need to get done each time — set up, break down tables and chairs, bring food if they can afford it, lead the introductions, or serve as group facilitator.

### TIPS

#### Men's Groups

• **Experiment with different times.** It's hard to find one time that works for everybody.

• **Experiment with different formats.** To keep things from getting stale, vary where you hold your meetings and how you organize your discussion.

• **Don't expect everybody to show up every time.** People will drift in and out based on their personal needs.

• **Let the men do it.** This is one where it's important to let the men take responsibility themselves. Make sure it is the men's program and build the agenda around their needs.

• **A men's group is never too small.** Group size can range from three to four to much larger. If you start with three or four, think of them as your core group upon which you will build.

• **Keep your meeting space private.** To assure men that they can talk as openly as they'd like, find a room for discussion where people won't be walking in and out and their conversation will not be overheard.

*The Father's Group at the Florence S. Brown Pre-K program in Rochester meets twice a month. One meeting is held during the day, so men working the night shift can attend; the other is held during the evening. The group is led by one of the fathers, with the agenda set by the men. Sometimes speakers are invited, but most of the time there is a free-floating discussion of whatever is on men's minds.*

## TIPS

### Curriculum for Parenting

• **Survey dads to see what questions they have.** Build your curriculum around their needs.

• **Be sure that your teaching and your curriculum are action oriented.** No one wants to listen to lectures for two hours. The activities should be hands-on as much as possible.

• **Draw upon the resources among the dads themselves.** You will probably find that most dads have feelings, opinions and some expertise when it comes to some of the topics.

---

Distribute the responsibilities so that everybody feels that he is contributing to the creation of the group.

## Activities for Men and Kids

Dads may not always like to attend meetings (so who does?) but they are suckers for having fun with their kids. One of the best ways for beginning to get dads more involved in your program is to create special opportunities for them to "get down" with their preschoolers.

Here are some activities other programs have used to get men and kids together:

■ **Saturday Morning Breakfast.** The Fairfax-San Anselmo Children's Center uses a leisurely

> "*B*elieve it or not, fathers love musical chairs," says Bossie Jackson, former assistant director for the New Dawn Head Start program in Newark, New Jersey. For his first father's workshop, Bossie set up an evening of games: chair bowling, alphabet bingo, piggyback races, musical chairs. "We had games so the fathers could interact with children," says Jackson. The activities get the fathers laughing and talking and then Bossie was able to talk to them about the hands-on things that are done in the early childhood setting. "Many men are under the impression that preschool learning is just play, not a learning process for children," Jackson says.

Saturday morning breakfast, once a month, with great success. Because the program serves predominantly low-income families, it uses government subsidized surplus food. Dads help out by preparing and serving and trying to get each other's kids to try a new cereal for a change. It gives everybody a chance to sit and talk and play without the pressures of the workday.

■ **Weekday Drop-off Breakfast.** Not every parent has Saturday off, so even a once-a-month breakfast is out of the question. Some programs offer

> *A*t the Early Learning Center of Temple Beth Sholom in Sarasota, Florida, dads have a choice of three different Daddy and Me modules. In the basic course, which meets in the evenings for an hour and fifteen minutes over a fourteen-week period, dads get a chance to share their parenting experiences with other fathers. The focus is on issues such as discipline, ways to play with babies and toddlers, feeding without fuss, and finding time for yourself. The second course, Daddy and Me - I, is oriented to fathers of babies from birth to 17 months, while Daddy and Me - II extends the age range from 18 to 36 months. A key focus in both groups is understanding what behavior to expect from young children and how to respond positively.

breakfasts for parents and kids during the week. They encourage parents to come early with their children and then to hang around after breakfast so they'll have a sense of what goes on at the program. While it doesn't have the leisurely pace of a Saturday morning, it's a good way for dads to get a glimpse of their children with other kids.

■ **Dinner and Drums.** Breakfast obviously isn't the only time to bring men and kids together. The PICA program in Hennepin County, Minnesota holds a male/child dinner and drum-making session which draws a huge crowd. In 1990, for example, 250 children showed up with 150 men to dine together and then make drums out of fruit juice cans. According to David Buckney, one of the head teachers in the program, "The men really loved it—some of them had never seen their child work independently."

## Curriculum for Parenting

Beyond ice breaking in a newly forming men's group, setting up "rap" or discussion groups, and creating activities that involve men with their children, you may want to offer a more structured curriculum for parenting.

It is almost a cliché that parents have never had formal training in how to be a parent. Many of the problems that parents have with children — and children with parents — may be related to their lack of basic information or alternative parenting role models.

A number of programs have developed the "curricular approach" to involve males in their programs. They vary somewhat in format and emphasis, but most include a mix of parenting skills and self-improvement topics.

■ **Three-Stage Curriculum.** The Minnesota Early Learning Design Young Dad's program in Minneapolis structures its curriculum into three stages, based on their experience with fathers' needs. Initial meetings are designed to get young men who are dads comfortable with meeting as a group . The meetings last for two hours. Once there is a certain comfort level in the group they move into discussions of the health needs of children and how children grow and develop. In the final stage of meetings they direct themselves to family management issues and help the men to develop personal growth goals and strategies.

■ **Parent-Child Communication.** The curriculum at the Dad and Me program of the Cambridge-Isanti school district in Minnesota emphasizes learning through parent-child interaction and communication. It uses television and videotapes as part of a group-discussion format that includes such topics as: relationships with our own fathers and mothers and how these impact on our relationships with our children; relationships with women, including sexuality; gender socialization; changing role of fathers; child development; family dilemmas and problem solving; child management; work-family balance and stress management; and communication skills.

■ **Saturdays With Dad.** Merry McNally, an early childhood educator with the Broome County Community College in New York, offers a four-week Saturday morning program for dads that combines hands on activities with their children—such as making ice cream—followed by a parenting talk session. The program, titled "Dad's Day," includes such topics as discipline, child development, and communication with your partner.

■ **Full Year.** In contrast to the four-week approach, San Antonio's Avance program offers a 33-week curriculum for dads. Topics covered during the two-hour evening sessions include: stages of parenthood, cultural pride, drug and alcohol abuse, learning to live without violence, and parents and language development. And the Central Nebraska Community Services program, a Head Start grantee, is working with the University of Nebraska at Kearney to develop a twelve-module curriculum for men that will cover such topics as the importance of the male role model to children, early childhood development, guidance and discipline, and nutrition.

■ **Open Forum.** THE CLUB in Boston holds weekly three-hour Open Forum meetings where men talk about such topics as resume writing, long-term career planning, how to achieve your dreams, entrepreneurship, substance abuse, sexually transmitted diseases, and anything else that the Hispanic and African-American men want to talk about. The meetings are led by director Roy Turner, outside visitors and speakers, and "mentors"—men from the community who are matched with club members.

## Special Recognition Events

How can you get moving towards greater father involvement when you feel overwhelmed by everything else you're trying to do? The easiest way is with the "one-shot deal," a special event that you offer once a year and make a lot of hoopla about so people pay attention.

The goal of the special event is to recognize the contribution that men make to the family, to acknowledge them and say "thank you." The most obvious time of year to do this is around Father's Day, but it doesn't have to be the only

*On the Saturday before Father's Day, the Cardinal Spellman Head Start in New York City hosts its annual all-day "fathers only" celebration. Teachers and children include the significant male friends in a morning of activities—painting, blocks, modeling with clay, and more. Then the men have a separate meeting with film and discussion. Afterwards everybody gets together for a barbecue.*

day. Here are some other ways to offer recognition at any time during the year:

■ **Men's Breakfast.** Offer to serve breakfast to dads or other men and their kids. This will allow you to catch many before they're off for school or work. Make sure that all staff and parents know that this is the men's breakfast, designed to acknowledge the role of men in their children's lives.

■ **Parents of the Month.** Once a month, select two or more parents to honor as "parents of the month." There should be an equal balance here between men and women. Post their pictures prominently for all to see when they walk in. If possible, display some text next to the photo that explains who the parents are and why they were selected. For example: "Tom is recognized for making sure Lynette got to the doctor this month"; "Sally is recognized for always being so cheerful when she comes to pick up Raphael." Good reasons abound if you keep in mind that the goal is to honor positive parenting. Over the course of the year, you will have honored at least twelve different men and twelve women; other parents will get the idea that you consider fathers to be an important part of the family.

■ **Service Awards.** This is like Parents of the Month but on a bigger scale. Once a year, recognize at least one man and one woman from your parent group for their contributions to the well-being of your program. This can be tied into a parents' meeting or other regularly scheduled event, or you can make it a freestanding affair. The point is to get the message across that both men and women contribute to your success.

## Family Events

Do men really need their own social events to "bond" with one another first? Do they *really* need special activities with their children? Wouldn't it be better to just get the whole family together, since that's the goal anyway?

Often, despite everybody's best intentions, family-oriented events get played out with mothers at the center of attention *and* responsibility. Mom is supposed to organize the kids, bring the food, and make sure everybody has a good time. Dad's responsibility is to show up!

## TIPS

### Special Recognition Events

• **Special events are good to stimulate thinking** about other types of recognition that can be given — to parents, staff, and administration.

• **Find out what other ideas parents have.** Ask parents, "What other types of recognition do you think we should be giving around here?"

• **Move beyond special events.** If you think of them as fulfilling some sort of obligation to "do something for the men around here," they will end up being both the beginning and the end.

• **Be sensitive to families with no father present.** Make sure your recognition is to men in general — that might include a grandfather, a neighbor, or a mother's friend.

• **Don't overdo it.** If you do too many events in too short a time frame, your special events will lose their "specialness."

• **Hold recognition events for mothers too.** Recognizing fathers and other men does not mean ignoring mothers. You will do so at your own peril!

*The twice-a-year overnight camping trips at the Fairfax-San Anselmo Children's Center are among the most popular events of the year. The trips are open to the whole family, not just the children enrolled in the center. But they are planned exclusively by men and they draw the participation of men who aren't otherwise involved in the center's Saturday morning breakfasts or other activities. "Among our Asian families this is a particularly popular event," says associate director Stan Seiderman. "Dads who won't come forward in other ways are right in there."*

## Skills Development

• **Literacy skills make it possible for parents to experience one of the great pleasures of parenthood — reading to their children.** But even non-readers, or beginning readers, can look at picture books with their children.

• **Be sure you're developing skills people can use to get a job.** Make sure there's a fit between your skills-development program and the labor market.

• **Survey parents to find out what skills they're interested in developing.** You may uncover surprises among both men and women. In Florida, for example, one program learned that its Hispanic mothers wanted to learn flower arranging, a skill which lent itself to the local economy.

• **Be sure to offer women the same skills development opportunities as men.** While reaching out with something of great psychological importance to men, don't ignore its importance and relevance to women.

An alternative to fathers-only events is to create events for the whole family *and* to give men extra incentives and responsibilities for being involved. There's almost no end to the center activities where men can play a special role. For example:

■ **Barbecues.** At the Camden Head Start, it has become a tradition for men to take charge of the annual picnic and barbecue. According to family involvement specialist Darryl Reeves, "Everybody says it's no big deal, and it isn't really, but the men love doing this. We get a great turnout."

■ **Pancake Breakfast.** The PICA Head Start in Minnesota uses a similar approach but a different meal. What started as a breakfast for men hosted by female staff has turned into a breakfast for men hosted by male staff and fathers or other men connected to the families. "It just evolved that way," says PICA director of health Bryan Nelson, "and now everybody looks forward to it."

■ **Game Night.** At the FOSPA program in St. Olaf, Minnesota, which is housed in an elementary school, dads take the lead in organizing games for the whole family in the gymnasium. Everybody is welcome to drop by and play kickball, basketball (with a three-foot-high basket), climb on the indoor jungle gym, or just run around and have a good time.

■ **Fundraisers.** No program ever has enough money. Because men are still brought up to think of themselves as providers, it's not surprising that they may feel particularly comfortable taking a role in your fundraising efforts.

## Skills Development

Men in our society are still expected, first and foremost, to be providers for their families. If they don't have the skills required to put bread on the table, men will often retreat from the family, and from other parts of the father role, out of a sense of shame and failure.

Some programs address the issue of employment head on. They get men involved by offering to develop the skills they need to get a job.

Here are some other ways to use education and training to bring more men into your program:

■ **Jobs Connection.** When Addison County's Parent Child Center wanted to involve the teenage fathers in their program, they decided they needed a "jobs" connection. Now the young men spend 20 hours each week learning how to detail cars or working in the program's packaging business.

In addition to job skills, they are learning how to keep a job by showing up on time and working cooperatively with others. The confidence they develop along with their skills translates into more comfort at spending time with their children at the center too.

*While four-year-olds are in their classrooms, mothers and fathers at the St. Bernardine's Head Start in Baltimore are in their classrooms, learning how to use computers, prepare resumes, conduct a job interview. This adult education program, open to the whole community, operates day and night. According to associate director Clarence Tucker, "It's the key to male involvement. Before we offered adult education, the only way you could bring men in was through the women. Now we have men coming in on their own. When they come to their own classes they see what the children are doing in their classes. That's the first step to getting them to parent meetings."*

■ **Child Development Training.** Your program offers a natural on-the-job training site for men to move into teaching positions. That's the approach taken by the Ounce of Prevention program in Chicago and by PICA in Minnesota; both are grooming men to work within their own programs or to move into other programs in the community. In Philadelphia, the Parent-Child Centers are training parents to be substitute teachers.

■ **Literacy.** Miami Valley's Child Development program in Ohio has encouraged male involvement through a weekly literacy program. In addition to learning to read, participants take regular trips to see how their new skills can be applied; after reading stories in the local newspaper, for example, they tour the newspaper offices to see how the daily edition is created. This has led many to continue their education by pursuing their G.E.D., starting college, or going into job-training programs.

**Chidren live and grow on positive feedback and the same is true for adults**

## CHAPTER
## 6

# Stage Four: Sustaining Male Involvement

Congratulations! If you've used some of the ideas in this book, you're on your way to increasing male involvement in your program. But how do you keep the momentum going? How do you build on your successes? Here's a set of strategies to keep things moving.

### Promote the Positive

Children live and grow with positive feedback, and it's no less true for adults. Recognizing the efforts and accomplishments of parents and staff who have been assisting with your male involvement initiatives will go a long way towards sustaining them.

There are lots of ways to give recognition, and lots of things to give recognition for. After all, it's not just major achievements that need praising, but the day-to-day activities that people are engaged in. Here are ways to use some simple tools that you may already have at hand:

■ **Newsletters.** If you've got a center newsletter, use it to feature brief and positive articles about your male involvement activities: for example, an interview with Mr. Smith who volunteered on the bus, a profile of Mr. Jiminez who is fixing tricycles, a description of the fun people had at the men's pancake breakfast. Your articles don't have to be long and they don't have to be

*On a recent spring day, we received a call from a very proud Darryl Reeves of Camden County Head Start. Darryl had just been notified of his selection as Parent Involvement Coordinator Of The Year by his region, mainly for his outreach to men. Despite what is often a difficult job with limited resources, this pumped him up and made him ready to keep going!*

45

## Promoting the positive

• **Put your best foot forward.** If three men showed up to your first men's group meeting, don't put out the word that "only three men showed up." Instead, write about the nucleus of men that's getting together, why they're so interested, and why the group will be valuable to others.

*In 1980, the Fairfax-San Anselmo Children's Center formed a Men's Planning Committee to figure out why so few fathers were engaged and what could be done to change that. Over a decade later, with a successful program in place, the Planning Committee still provides the vehicle for regular, albeit informal, evaluation of what else needs to be done and what could be done better.*

headline news; as long as you're paying attention, your readers will too. You might even consider a regular Men's Corner, an idea that Stan Seiderman uses in his newsletter at the Fairfax-San Anselmo Children's Center.

■ **Flyers.** If you don't have a newsletter, you can use flyers to spread the good word. You're probably doing that already to announce meetings. Make it a regular habit to use the back of each announcement to tell parents something positive that's happening at your program.

■ **Newspaper Articles.** If you live in a small town, your local newspaper is probably hungry for stories. It's still considered relatively unusual—and therefore "newsworthy"—for men to be involved with young children. If an article does get written, be sure to make copies for distribution to your board, staff and parents, and post a copy prominently on your bulletin board.

■ **Photos.** Just as photos help create a "father-friendly" environment, they will help sustain it. Display photos of any of your male involvement activities in prominent places, and you will reinforce the progress you've made.

■ **Honors.** Some businesses recognize an "employee of the month" and post his or her

picture for customers to see. You can borrow that technique for your staff and parents. Use it to value contributions of all sorts, including male involvement activities. If you post a picture, write a paragraph or two next to it explaining why that person has been selected.

## Assess Your Progress Regularly

You won't really know if you are sustaining your program unless you take stock of where you've been and where you want to go. Moreover, you're more likely to make things happen if you measure them. The process of assessment will help keep you focused.

Here are some steps to take for assessment:

■ **Set Up an Assessment Team.** It helps to look at your program from the perspective of different participants: parents, staff and board as well as men and women. Set up a team with representation from each significant group in your program, and ask them to work together to determine the progress you're making. Each representative can collect information from his or her constituency.

■ **Use the Male Involvement Audit.** The male involvement audit provided in Chapter One of this book offers one way to get started with your assessment. If you have used it already to determine whether or not you have a father-friendly environment, you can use it again to see what sort of progress you've made. It is also important to adapt the audit for any particular needs or features of your program.

■ **Take a Look Outside.** While it's important to measure progress against your specific program goals, it lends perspective to look at your program in comparison to other programs. It can also give you new ideas for program development on male involvement. Attending national and regional meetings of the National Association for the Education of Young Children, the National Head Start Association, and other early childhood groups is one way to do this. But you can also start in your own backyard by visiting, observing, and interviewing the director at other programs in your area. If you have a local inter-agency group, set aside a meeting or part of a meeting to compare efforts on male involvement.

■ **Build on Your Small Steps.** After they do an assessment, some programs get stuck because they don't

**Display photos of any of your male involvement activities in prominent places, and you will reinforce the progress you've made.**

think they've made enough progress—and therefore won't make any at all. Others think they have to do everything at once. Avoid these self-defeating attitudes by identifying the small steps you have taken and then determining what small step you can take next. Before you know it, those small steps will have led you to cover a lot of ground!

## Cultivate Your Leadership

Most programs get started because of the initiative of one person or a small group of people. But if they get too dependent on or identified with that one person, they can founder if he or she leaves. To sustain your program it is important to develop your leadership—the ability of one or more people to take responsibility and empower others. Here are some ways to cultivate the leadership potential in your program:

■ **Identify Future Leaders Now.** Leadership isn't something to think about for "later on" — when your program is in transition or when current leaders leave. It takes time to cultivate leadership, time for newcomers (staff or parents) to feel comfortable enough with your program, and time for people to realize that their colleagues look at them as leaders. So stay on the alert for people who have that extra spark of commitment, initiative, passion or intelligence about your program.

■ **Spread the Responsibility.** Don't rely on one or a few people to get things done. Give people a chance to show their leadership by sharing the responsibility. And don't assume that leaders are the ones who talk the most at meetings; future leadership talent may reside in people who are on the quiet side. To make sure he's giving everybody a chance, Clarence Tucker rotates the discussion leader every week for the Men's Group at the St. Bernardine's Head Start.

■ **Praise Others' Initiative.** Draw out the leadership potential of your group by affirming others when they show their initiative or follow-through.

■ **Ask Parents for Help.** Some of your future leaders may not yet be involved in your activities. Ask parents about who isn't showing up and which members of the group, in their opinion, could be tapped for a fuller role — Then

*The Men's Group at the Fairfax-San Anselmo Children's Center has been operating for over a decade under the stewardship of associate director Stan Seiderman. But when asked if Stan is critical to the group's continuation, participants quickly say, "No. It's important for somebody to step into Stan's role, but it doesn't have to be Stan." Does Stan Seiderman feel insulted that he's replaceable? Not at all. He's created the feeling that the group is more important than any single member, and enabled others to feel they can keep it going.*

approach that person by saying, "I hear you'd be a terrific addition to our efforts." The recognition just may land you a future leader.

## Build a Network

Being part of a network of programs committed to furthering male involvement is very empowering — and sustaining.

But there are other ways, short of creating a statewide alliance, to begin building a support network.

■ **Find a Local Program Partner.** If you find one other program that shares your goals, you've got the beginning of a network. That was Bossie Jackson's approach in Newark, New Jersey, when he was a teacher at the New Dawn Day Care. After sponsoring a successful father-child night at his center, Bossie teamed with Johnnie Meyers, director of Full Gospel Day Care, to organize an event co-sponsored by both centers. Given its success, they're now approaching other centers in the city and are slowly growing their own support network.

■ **Work with Local Associations.** Local chapters of the National Association for the Education of Young Children and the National Head Start Association are always looking for ways to promote inter-agency cooperation. In Cleveland, for example, the AEYC sponsors a Men in Child Care Committee that has conducted a city and statewide survey about male early childhood teachers. It is using the survey results as a basis for future planning. Ask your local chapter to serve as the forum to bring other professionals together and you may have the beginning of your network.

*In Minnesota, staff from programs from Minneapolis to St. Cloud have joined together to form the Minnesota Fathering Alliance. They meet a few times a year to share ideas and are in touch regularly by telephone. They have even hosted a conference on father involvement and written a book,* Working with Fathers. *When any one of them feels he's facing an uphill struggle, he knows where to turn for moral support!*

# Model Programs

CHAPTER
**7**

# Job Training and Parent Education

## ADDISON COUNTY PARENT-CHILD CENTER, INC.

**Location:** Middlebury, VT

**Clients:** 150 rural, low-income teenage parents or prospective parents

**Services:** child care, resource & referral, parent education

**Staff:** 21, including 6 men

**Funding:** Federal and state government; private grants

*Addison County involves teenaged fathers by providing them with work, job training and parent education. The young men operate an on-site car refurbishing business, "Dads' Detailing," and through a combination of support groups and classroom instruction, learn about their infants and toddlers under the supervision of child care-givers. The program reaches out to other young men in a cooperative program with area high schools to identify and educate teenagers who have a high risk of pregnancy.*

## Background

The Green Mountains loom to the east; Lake Champlain is a short ride to the west. Every day three vans travel over 150 miles through one of the poorest counties in Vermont to bring entire families — most with white teen parents — to the new wood frame building that sits in the valley with Middlebury College. It's a place for children to receive care, and for parents to learn to be parents.

Until 1980, parents meant moms. That's when outreach worker Jordan Engel, a Middlebury graduate with a master's in speech pathology, noticed that the dads were being left out. He urged the program administrators and governing board to pursue and engage the husbands and boyfriends of the young moms in the program.

Early attempts to teach these high-school dropouts about infants and toddlers failed until Jordan and staff member Gerry Slager discovered that what these sixteen-year-olds really needed was jobs. In order to get jobs they needed skills. So in 1989 the Addison PCC launched a car detailing shop that trains the men, lets them work cooperatively, and encourages them to talk about their lives as teen fathers.

## Cars and Kids

For two hours each day the six young men in the program refurbish cars of local citizens to an almost new condition for $60, well below the standard price for such a service but enough to make a small profit for the program. Black corduroy "Dads' Detailing" caps atop their heads, they energetically wash, wax and polish, learning to come to work on time and to work under adult supervision. They also learn that work is a team effort, with each person taking a share of responsibility.

The rest of the day they are in the center, designed purposely to provide a feeling of family, where they assist with their children and learn about child development or do kitchen and maintenance work. The rooms are light and airy, painted in soft pastels, with tables and chairs to congregate and nutritious food always available—an important feature for families whose daily diets tend to consist of fast foods and sweets.

Staff are everpresent in the five preschool

At the center, the men assist with their children and learn about child development.

classrooms and make it clear that these young men and women are valued. "This is a place for them to start over," says one staff member. "Adult relationships have been rocky for many of them."

Each of the men receives $1.00 an hour for any work, whether detailing cars, cooking or cleaning in the center, or learning about his child in one of the classrooms. The additional

Through "Dads Detailing" (left), men learn that work involves team effort and responsibility.

**Being involved with children in positive ways helps build men's self-esteem.**

men and rebuilding their self esteem."

In one recent meeting the two psychologists pressed Walter on why he hadn't asked the other men in the group to help him move to a new apartment. Walter, annoyed by the question, said, "I thought they might be too busy to help me. I'll find a way to do it myself." One by one the other men said, "I'll help." "Why don't you use my pickup?" Unwilling to trust others in the past, Walter was getting the message that it was safe to reach out.

The men's group back at the center is led by Jordan and Gerry, now in his forties but a father at 19. It focuses on what it is like to be a father but includes talk about jobs, cars and recreational activities. "Any friends I have are here," says Robert. Brian admits that the program has had a big impact on him. "I used to be only interested in wild parties. I'm a lot calmer now. I've learned to talk about my feelings. My wife and I tend to talk out our problems more now."

According to Gerry and Jordan, men will likely be turned off by a program if they feel isolated in what they perceive to be a "women's place." It's important for them to meet in small groups, work together, play volleyball together. But the group size grows from six to thirty-two when the men combine with the mothers once a week to continue their conversations about relationships, children and other topics. One of the myths that has been destroyed is the notion that young men are uncommunicative. "You should see them in group," says Jordan, "they talk about everything."

### Outreach

The center also operates high school workshops to talk about relationships and pregnancy prevention. Michael, one of the outreach staff of the center, regularly meets with over 100 junior and senior high students in four of the area's secondary schools. He works with school guidance staff to find "pda's"—teenaged couples who are exhibiting public displays of affection. Michael then holds teen couples' groups that meet four times each month. Michael and the guidance counselor run the meeting where questions about relationships are explored.

$25 a week is an important source of income that does not affect their welfare check. According to Jordan Engel, director of the program, it is also one of the reasons that they continue to come back.

### Community for Men

In addition to their car detailing and time with their children, the young men spend five hours each week in two different support groups. One, led by psychologists from a local mental health center, is held at the car detailing shop, the other at the center. "These men come to the program with very low self esteem," says co-director Cheryl Mitchell. "Staff spend much of the time in the group attempting to build trust among the

### Contact

Cheryl Mitchell and Sue Harding
Co-Directors
11 Seminary Street
Middlebury, VT 05753
Telephone: (802) 388-3171

# CHAPTER
## 8
# Curriculum For Dads

*A*vance offers fatherhood classes to dads over a 33-week period. Up to 20 men per week meet together at the center to discuss such topics as child growth and development, handling stress, learning to live without violence, and childhood illnesses. They study for their G.E.D. and learn to speak English in E.S.L. classes. The program also joins the men with the mothers in the program, who meet separately with their own curriculum, for family outings, cultural and sporting events, first aid classes, etc.

### Background

Avance, a private non-profit agency to strengthen and support families, was founded in 1973 by native San Antonian, Dr. Gloria G. Rodriguez. It began as a program to help women in the Hispanic community to develop parenting and personal skills through a structured curriculum of classes offered in housing projects throughout San Antonio. It now provides educational programs and direct services to nearly 3,000 predominantly low-income Hispanic adults and children per year and conducts research and training programs.

For its first fifteen years, the focus of Avance was on women. In 1987, Rodriguez began to notice that in a large number of single parent families, men were being kicked out of the household so that women could qualify for welfare benefits. In an Hispanic culture that stressed the importance of manhood, men were being stripped of their manhood, and many turned to drugs and alcohol. With limited education and no job skills, many were lacking in self-esteem and unable to assume the "head of the family" position demanded by the culture. By contrast, the women participating in Avance's nine-month mothers' program were motivated; they were learning English, earning their high school equivalency diplomas and going on to productive lives. According to Rodriguez, "The mother was growing, the child

**AVANCE**

**Location:** San Antonio, TX.

**Services:** 4000 individuals, 2000 children

**Diversity:** 99% Hispanic, 1% African-American

**Funding:** 3.5 million annual budget

was growing and the father was staying behind."

With funding from the A.L. Mailman and the Hasbro Foundations, Avance launched a fatherhood program focused on Hispanic and African-American males, to preserve the family unit and to help the father grow personally, educationally and economically. It operates under the direction of former teacher Isaac Cardenas, himself a product of the barrio who had chosen to continue to live in the community. Through a variety of means, the program teaches some 60 men a year parenting and personal skills, encourages their involvement with their children and strengthens their relationships with their spouses.

## A Curriculum for Fathers

At the heart of the fatherhood program is the weekly two-hour meeting, held at an early childhood center in a building provided by the San Antonio Housing Authority. Over a 33-week period, Isaac Cardenas and his associate, Rubin Torrez, cover topics such as parenting, Latino family life, cultural pride, learning to live without violence, child abuse, relaxation techniques, drug and alcohol abuse and nutrition. Though guided by three curriculum workbooks, the discussions are wide-ranging, since the program also provides a place for community and support.

One man attending a recent meeting had brought along his three-year-old because his wife was attending her own weekly meeting. The mothers' and fathers' groups have been separated because, at this early stage of the development of the project, the administrators feel that each group needs to develop its own group identity and social support network. As one man said, "Things are different when you put men and women together in a group." David, age 24, came reluctantly to the group because his wife prodded him into it. Now he is working on his G.E.D. and has learned to cope with his two children. He comes regularly, even though he puts in 50 hours a week working several jobs.

John, one of the few African-American members, was in the midst of a divorce when he joined the group. "This group has given me a place where I can get together to talk with other men. We can share our problems here," says John. Another man explains, to group laughter, how he learned to discipline his children. "I used to spank them every time they got into trouble. Now I just take away their Nintendo game!"

Of the 60 men enrolled in the program during the 1990-1991 year, 15 had been referred to Avance by the court system, most in connection with family issues: domestic violence, child custody disputes, child abuse, neglect, or school truancy. As a condition of his parole, Raymond has been attending fatherhood classes; the judge will take Raymond's regular attendance in the program into consideration when she decides whether or not he retains custody of his children, and program coordinator Isaac Cardenas is required to make periodic reports to the court on his behalf.

**Working with children on a regular basis helps build close bonds.**

**Outings to the local state park are taken to strengthen the family unit.**

## Eyes and Ears

Johnny, the van driver who brings men to and from the fatherhood program is, as Isaac Cardenas says, "its eyes and ears." But not just because he's from the community, he is able to recruit men and discreetly inform Isaac and Ruben about problems in their lives. Johnny is also a graduate of the program.

After he lost his job with the 7-Up Bottling Company, Johnny worked odd jobs in the San

**Many of the outings and events are eye-openers to the men.**

## The Family Outing

Every year in April San Antonio celebrates Fiesta, a gala event with parades, outdoor crafts displays, and an array of ethnic foods. For the past two years, the fatherhood program has set up its own tables and chairs in a park in a prime location. "For many of the men and their families," says Cardenas, "this was the first time they had been downtown or to a parade." To strengthen the family unit the program has sponsored pre-Thanksgiving dinners for families, an outing at the local Holiday Inn, trips to the local library and museums, and walks through the local state parks. For many of the men these events are real eye-openers. For example, Francisco says, "I would never have thought of doing these types of activities, but now I plan to return on my own with my family." David, another father, says, "I never knew such places existed, and are free of charge or are a small fee to enter." Yet another father, Alex, is enthusiastic about the field trips: "Hey Isaac, you know that park you took us to? Well, I took my family back there with my other relatives and we had a great time!"

## The Scouting Component

When Cardenas' early attempts to recruit fathers were not yielding the results he expected, he began a Cub Scout pack for boys and a Girl Scout troop for girls and asked men to participate with their children. The groups meet weekly in the Avance center in the heart of San Antonio's West Side. Some men come occasionally, others almost every week. For Alex Cruz, who installs water conditioning equipment, the Tuesday night Cub Scout meetings have helped him to grow closer to his stepchild, Isaac. "I figured that it was time to get involved with what Isaac was doing," says Alex. "It doesn't matter if you're the natural father or not. You need that deep emotional bond."

## Contact

Dr. Gloria G. Rodriguez, Executive Director
Isaac Cardenas, Program Director
301 South Frio Street - Suite 310
San Antonio, TX 78207
Telephone: (210) 270-4630
Fax: (210) 270-4612

Antonio area. His wife started going to Avance for classes and convinced him to try some fatherhood classes. "It taught me how to care for my family, and how to care for myself as a person," Johnny says. Eventually he took the van driving position and now plans to go to school to be an EMS technician " The men trust me enough to tell me their problems," he says. "I can help them because I was where many are at. I compare the way I was and the way I am now."

### Building Trust

Sometimes men are reluctant to come to the weekly fatherhood classes. Many have had negative experiences with schools and find the classroom an intimidating place. Others, whose immigration status is uncertain, are fearful that public exposure in a classroom will increase their chances of being turned in to government authorities. "It takes quite a while to build trust," according to Cardenas.

But just because a man is reluctant to come to the program doesn't mean the program won't come to him. Both Isaac and Ruben go to the homes to teach. Ruben, for example, has been working with Arturo, an undocumented alien who crossed the Mexican border to reunite with his family. Arturo has had marital problems and has been suicidal, but is receiving home tutoring from Ruben using the workbook from the regular fatherhood classes. Isaac and Ruben both feel that if a father feels uncertain about the program, it is better to meet with him at home in a place where he feels he has some control.

- **Assume that all men can be reached** no matter what their background, attitude, limitations or age.
- **Look for opportunities** to meet specific needs. Once a man knows you are there to help him, you begin to build trust.
- **Follow up.** If you have invited a man to come to an event and he doesn't show up, call or visit to find out why.
- **Be flexible.** Hours of classes need to change with the seasons to accommodate overtime work schedules.
- **Hire staff who are sensitive** to the needs of the dads and can relate to them linguistically and culturally.
- **Stick to the "men only" concept.** The men will not feel intimidated and may open up better without the presence of women.
- **Hold classes in the community.** Be sure to provide for transportation and child care.
- **Education and later training** such as E.S.L. and G.E.D., which can lead to a job or a better job, is very important.

## CHAPTER

# Beyond the Father's Day Celebration

### CARDINAL SPELLMAN HEAD START

**Location:** New York, N.Y.

**Children:** 125 3-and 4-year-olds, 18 % with special needs

**Families:** 62% single parent, 21% teen parent, 90% below poverty

**Diversity:** 50% Latino, 20% Asian, 8% African-American, 22% various Caucasian

*W hat started as an annual Father's Day event has expanded to a variety of techniques to recruit and involve men. Staff actively use "lobby time" and parent meetings to seek out fathers who later can often be found sharing their time and talents in the center. A reward system called "Lucky Bucks" encourages participation and a relationship with a local high school brings young men into regular contact with children in Head Start classrooms.*

### Background

At this 25-year-old program the idea of involving more men started with a conversation between director Joanne Milano and two of her senior colleagues. Each had noticed the growth in the number of children attending Head Start from single mother-headed households and that Father's Day came and went every year without notice. As Joanne remembers it, "It started just

like that, with one of us saying, 'Why don't we have a Father's Day celebration?'"

That conversation led to a now annual event which draws men from over 50 percent of the center's families. Sensitive from the beginning to the possibility of the lack of a biological father in the child's life, all men were invited: fathers, guardians, uncles, older brothers, even male neighbors if they were important in the child's life. But the push to involve fathers has expanded to become an almost daily event.

### Program Accessibility

"We make a point of having parent meetings scheduled so that we can get a.m. and p.m. parents," says Joanne Milano.

Mr. Chan, a young restaurant worker recently arrived from Hong Kong, benefits from this type of scheduling. While his wife is at work, he brings four-year-old Manshan to the center and attends the a.m. parent meeting before going to his job in a local restaurant.

Staff are very sensitive to the need to alter meeting schedules if they conflict with parents' schedules, and will schedule meetings in the evening. They also make it clear in announcements that both mother and father are invited and that parents can bring younger children too.

## Recruitment

The apparent absence of the father or other significant male figure in the family doesn't stop the Cardinal Spellman staff. The intake interviewer is trained to ask, "Is there any male that the child has a steady relationship with?" The same question gets asked informally by social services staff in the lobby, by teachers outside of the classroom and during home visits. When Father's Day comes around staff are aggressive about looking for any male who is important in the child's life.

Social services staff are especially conscientious about making contact with fathers when they drop their children off and are "in the lobby." They talk to men about their children, inform them of future events, and actively call upon them to contribute their skills to the program. It is the active asking that staff feel makes a difference. It also reflects the common understanding that involvement of men can take many forms.

## Student Interns

When visitors circulate among the center's five classrooms they are likely to see lots of men. Second-semester seniors from Manhattan's Regis High School serve full-time, full-day internships in the classroom as part of their Christian service.

James, who is white, 17, and a former Head Start child himself, chose to volunteer in Head Start even though he will be studying computer science in college in the fall because Head Start "teaches you about little kids and it teaches you things about yourself—like patience." Marty, also white and 17, points to the fact that many of the children don't have male figures in their lives and, like James, thinks the children need adults who can spend time with them. "Sometimes one of the children will run up to me and ask me to read a story, just like that," says Marty. "Kids need adults around who can do this."

## The Annual Outing

Once a year the center hosts its annual "Fathers Only" event. Notices are sent out to families in

several languages inviting fathers and other men to "share in your child's pre-school experience."

On one recent Saturday, 32 fathers, grandfathers, uncles, and male friends of the family spent a full day in celebration with their children. The day began with the children and fathers together in the classrooms. Assisted by classroom teachers, they painted, played with blocks, modeled with clay, traced the bodies of the children on large white pieces of paper, and experimented with the IBM computers that are in each of the classrooms.

Then, while children stayed behind in the classroom with their teachers, the fathers joined Milano and other staff to watch a videotape, "Head Start: A Nation's Pride" and to talk about the importance of fathers in children's lives. Many Head Start fathers stood up in the meeting and talked about the importance of

High school interns provide positive role-models for the children.

A grandfather helps his graddaughter pick out a pumpkin.

## TIPS

• **Prepare your staff for male involvement.** Many, particularly those who have been around awhile, may be unused to and uncomfortable with this idea. There may be some initial discomfort until the staff is convinced about the need for male involement and how it can be important for children.

• **Be convinced yourself before you try to convince others** about involving more men. If you are not convinced, you won't convince others.

• **Go slowly.** Try a few "fathers only" events before plunging into a full program.

Head Start for them and their children.

One father, who set aside Saturday religious observances to attend the event was clearly surprised at the large attendance. "I think Head Start is wonderful for the family," he announced. Another father of five had never done much with his child before Head Start: "Now we play together with puzzles." Jose, a great-grandfather, came to the event because, "there isn't a dad in my grandchild's home." Mr. Wong, a grandfather from Hong Kong attends the annual father's event, parent meetings, and volunteers as a lunch assistant, because he is retired and because granddaughter Melinda likes having him in the center. "I come," he says, "because I care about my grandchild."

The day closes with a backyard barbeque where children and men share a meal together.

### Cultural Diversity

The wide diversity of ethnic and religious cultures of the families being served is an asset at Cardinal Spellman. The center staff and parent group look for ways of selecting and involving fathers and other males, often using the father's culture as an ally. Chinese and Bengali men, proud of their heritage of fine food, might be asked to prepare food for a Head Start function. A Hispanic man might be asked to talk to children about a Spanish holiday. A Polish father, who is also a carpenter, might be asked to do repair work in the center. The center staff have an unwritten rule: Find out what the parents are proud of, and use it to get them involved.

The center also has different definitions of family. Recently, Eduardo became the first male policy council chairperson in the program's history. Eduardo, who makes and sells jewelry, spends many hours at the center. He lives across the street in an apartment building that looks down over the center, which is located on the lower east side of Manhattan within a yellow masonry-faced community center operated by Catholic Charities. He attends the once a month parent meetings, both the a.m. and the p.m. and has vigorously taken on the chief fund raiser role. However, Eduardo is not a natural parent to four-year-old Joshua. To Joshua, he is "daddy pop." When Joshua's mother and father died, Eduardo moved in with William, Joshua's uncle and legal guardian. Together, they share household and child rearing duties. With this move, Joshua got a second "daddy" and Head Start got two devoted parent volunteers. Eduardo volunteers in the classroom, attends both the annual Mother's Day at the center (the Head Start mothers call him "Mr.Mom"), and the annual Father's Day function. William can be seen assisting with lunch time duties and accompanying the children on class trips.

### Contact

Joanne Milano, Director
137 East Second Street
New York, NY 10009
Telephone: (212) 677-7766
Fax: (212) 995-8537

**Men's participation with the chidren can take many forms.**

JAMES LEVIN

## CHAPTER
## 10
# Mentoring to Young Men

*I*n THE CLUB, *older professional men serve as mentors to African-American and Latino men between the ages of 18 and 25 who are considered high risk. Though not linked to an early childhood program, THE CLUB's weekly training in life skills and career planning can be readily adapted.*

### Background
"Men were getting squeezed out—especially young black and Hispanic males."

That's what prompted the 1989 sponsorship of THE CLUB, says administrator Jay Ostrower, by the Center for Jobs Education and Career Training, part of Action for Boston Community Development (ABCD), the city's anti-poverty agency. During the mid-1980s, Ostrower and his colleagues saw government funding for job training decline by 70%, along with the number of jobs not requiring a college education. The funding that was available for training had shifted to welfare recipients, most of whom were women. It was a situation destined to increase the likelihood that young black and Latino men would be involved with the criminal justice system.

The fledgling program is supported by a $241,000 grant from the Department of Health and Human Services, through a Demonstration Partnership Program administered by the Office

of Community Services. "Our goal," says director Roy Turner, is to "combine character building and personal support with efforts to improve employment and income, increase education and job skills while assisting members with social services and other life issues." It calls on men of color, generally professional men with standing in the community, as mentors to low income men between the ages of 18 and 25.

### THE CLUB: A Support Group for Men
On a Monday evening in June, a meeting of THE CLUB is about to begin. Roy Turner sits making telephone calls at a reception desk while members and mentors drift in. Turner, who is having a telephone conversation about starting a basketball team with THE CLUB members, interrupts his conversation periodically to greet each club member, asking questions, passing them notes, sharing information about job contacts he has made on their behalf during the past week. The mood of these encounters is light. Conversation and jokes come easily to Roy and CLUB members.

When he is finished talking on the telephone, Roy has a lengthy conversation with one of the early arrivals, Victor, a Hispanic man in his early 20s who has brought two other young Hispanic men with him. They talk about the three books, suggested by Turner, that Victor plans to read

<table>
<tr><td>THE CLUB<br>Location: Boston, MA</td></tr>
<tr><td>Services: enrollment over 100, 45 active members</td></tr>
<tr><td>Diversity: 65% African-American, 35% Latino</td></tr>
</table>

## TIPS

•**Be sure the first visit is positive.** The men you're trying to reach may have had negative experiences with other social-service agencies.

•**Network with other agencies** to seek referrals of men who could benefit from your services.

•**By definition, a club is a group of people who meet regularly to share common interests,** a membership organization that sets its own rules, organizes its own activities, recruits new members, and provides support to those who belong to the group. Be sure to include these elements when starting your club.

•**Don't limit membership to clients only.** Include others who have skills to share.

•**Individualize your services.** Remember: Each member comes with his own unique needs.

•**Provide literacy training and some financial assistance.** Generally, CLUB members receive $100-200 at the completion of each phase of the Individualized Career and Life Plan.

next week on vacation. This is a success story: Victor was a "walk-in"—unemployed, just released from prison for selling drugs. He enrolled, but it was a long time before he started coming to meetings. According to Turner, "Victor was very cautious." But with Roy's encouragement, Victor finally did attend, and the second meeting hooked him. Through the program, Victor got a part-time job taking the federal census. He liked the job but lost it when he got into an argument with his supervisor. At one of the meetings, Victor met Miranda, a health education coordinator at Alianza Hispana, a local social service agency. Miranda is one of the program's mentors and was instrumental in getting Victor a full-time job as a community outreach worker.

The meeting begins at 6:00 p.m. and by this time there are 16 men — 4 mentors and 12 members — sitting in a circle. Led by Roy Turner, the focus of the group promptly shifts to Ronald who is black, 22, with a badly bloodshot eye. "I had real bad attitude when I first came here," says Ronald, relating the story about his eye. He was driving his father's car in a section of Boston and was stopped at a traffic light. Two men opened the door, put him in a chokehold, and held a 9 mm pistol to his head. Ronald lost $60.00 in the incident, but he's proud that he didn't reach under the seat and pull out the pistol that was taped and shoot his assailants. Before joining THE CLUB, he would have done this. Now he laughs. "Two years ago I would have gotten killed—just another black—just a statistic." The group nods its approval though a few of the members admit that they might not have shown the same control. Ronald is another of THE CLUB's success stories. Through the program he has gotten job training and a job and will be entering a local university in the fall.

Throughout the evening members share their stories. Rashid, another 22-year-old, came to the program homeless and jobless. Through Turner's efforts he found temporary housing, a part-time job, and a lot of support. "Everybody in this group has helped me in some way," he says.

### Mentors
Four mentors are present this evening, all older black men: an expediter in a local factory, a graphic artist, a banker, and a physician who works in the AIDS unit in a local hospital. For Frank, the factory supervisor, what seemed like "a good idea" has become a responsibility: "We adults have a responsibility to these young black men. They're dying out there. We have to redirect them in positive directions." Although

Frank has been attending for 14 months, he has not yet been formally linked with a member. Roy Turner explains that it takes time for relationships to form — they can't be forced. But once it's clear that there is a match, both mentor and member actually sign a written "match contract," agreeing to meet no fewer than 10 hours a month and to attend club meetings and counseling sessions. In addition, mentors are required to file a monthly "contact profile," giving a narrative review of the previous month's contact with the member. Turner points out that the difficulty of finding enough mentors has led THE CLUB to develop a team mentoring structure.

Gareth, a 32-year-old business development officer for a local bank who grew up in the projects of New York City, was successfully matched with 23-year-old George. "I'm tired of hearing about what is wrong with these young men," he says. "I've decided to do something about it." Gareth feels he has grown from the experience. "It keeps me in touch. I used to be like some of these young men. One person can make a difference!" The man he mentors, George, used to sell drugs but now holds a well-paying job as a turnpike collector, and has attended every CLUB meeting to date.

### Life and Parenting Skills
The final portion of the two hour meeting is a slide presentation and discussion on sexually transmitted diseases, led by Dr. John Rich, a long time mentor who has collaborated on a number of projects to provide health services for men who don't have health insurance. Tonight's meeting addresses the results of unsafe sexual practices. Previous meetings have included such topics as resume preparation, goal setting, entrepreneurship, owning your own business, substance abuse, spirituality and religion.

One of THE CLUB's goals is to help men develop the skills needed to become more effective fathers. In a controlled study, researchers attempted to determine if THE CLUB improved parenting behavior among members compared with a similar group of men who applied for membership, but did not ultimately attend. The researchers found members were more likely to live at home with the mother of the child, see the child on a more regular basis, and provide financial support to the family.

### Contact
Roy Turner, Program Director
100 Shawmut Ave.
Boston, MA 02118
(617) 357-6000 x 784

## CHAPTER
## 11
# Using the Public Schools

*T*hrough its statewide early childhood family education program, Minnesota offers information and support to all parents and their children from birth to kindergarten. But it's not just moms who show up at the local elementary schools for weekly parent/child groups and parent group discussions. A special Dad and Me component, usually offered during the evenings, provides a regular time and place for fathers to get together with their kids and to learn from other men— and women. "It's a commitment that you make," says one dad who has been with the program for three years. "I'm very disappointed if I can't make it."

### Background

First proposed by the Minnesota legislature in 1971, the early childhood family education (ECFE) concept is quite simple: find a cost-effective way to offer education and support to all parents—regardless of income—as soon as their children are born. Make these services available locally by using public school space, and staff them with licensed parent educators and early childhood teachers. All this is to encourage healthy family development and reduce the potential costs of later remediation.

The idea was tested and refined from 1974 to 1984, through a series of 34 pilot programs funded by the legislature and coordinated by the Minnesota Council on Quality Education. In

1984, the legislature made it possible for any school district with a Community Education program to establish an ECFE program. The programs are funded through a combination of state aid and local taxes, which can be supplemented by registration fees or funds from other sources.

By the early '90s, almost 400 out of 435 school districts were designated Community Education districts, eligible to levy taxes for ECFE, and over 300 districts were offering ECFE programs.

### Dad and Me

Dads have never been excluded from ECFE. But according to Bob Brancale, ECFE coordinator in Minneapolis, "When we started as a pilot program in 1976 we just weren't reaching men, we even had mothers signing up the dads but they just wouldn't show."

So Brancale and his colleague Ron Gustafson decided to appeal to the "jock" in men. They rented a gym and invited men to come to a "Dad's Night Out" — floor hockey and volleyball without the kids, followed by refreshments. "After we exhausted talking about all the sports franchises in Minneapolis, somebody asked what the wives did at the ECFE program. When we told them what we did, three of the 15 guys showed some interest. We later ended up going door-to-door with these guys handing out flyers about the "Dad and Me" program.

After three years, Dad and Me had grown

**DAD AND ME**

**Location:** White Bear Lake, MN.

**Services:** 450 familes

**Diversity:** predominantly white; 16% low income; 10% single parents; 9% teen parents

**Funding:** local community

In the Dad and Me program, an effort is made to enable men and their children to spend special time together.

from one class with six men to four classes with 85, by word of mouth and steady publicity. Brancale took lots of pictures to hang around the center — so moms would know about the dads program — and put them in all ECFE publications. In 1984, he organized a Saturday conference where Lou Nanne, president of the North Stars hockey team, talked about how he was raised, appealing to the "jock" element in the dads worked again — 180 men showed up.

By the early '90s, ECFE was offering 125 classes per week in Minneapolis of which five were Dad and Me. While most participants are middle-income, the program also reaches men of varied backgrounds. Eric Ziegler, a group leader in North Minneapolis, recently had a group that included a man whose significant other is in jail; he wanted to keep custody and wanted to be a "good dad" and known as "a man had just come out of jail and took custody of his kids from his wife, a chronic alcoholic."

Other communities are also adapting their ECFE programs to reach to men. White Bear Lake, a largely middle-income suburb northeast of St. Paul, started its first Dad and Me class in 1986. Now its 55 parent-child groups each week include three Dad and Me evening classes, and nine other evening classes consist of about 30 percent men.

"We've never had to market this," says Lowell Johnson, the early childhood teacher/parent educator who leads most of the Dad and Me groups in White Bear Lake. "Most men get in because their wives sign them up or encourage them to sign up. But once the men come, they stick with us. They even want us to extend the program past kindergarten."

### A Man to Relate To

According to Shirley Trossen, principal and director of early childhood programs in White Bear Lake, one reason for the success of Dad and Me is:

"We had a male offering Dad and Me from the beginning. The women staff were able to work with a male preschool teacher and knew he would relate to the Dad and Me class. A lot of people want Lowell's class or want their husbands to have Lowell's class."

Lowell Johnson stands out from his female colleagues because of his lanky six-foot frame and his hobbies. As a hunter, he's off in the woods with his rifle at the beginning of deer season. As a small-scale farmer, he's up at sunrise everyday to feed his animals.

Like his female colleagues, however, Johnson spends much of his time creating a space where parents and their children can spend some very special time together, and where parents can learn from one another.

### Play Time

At 5 p.m. on a Tuesday night, in a bright, well-lit early childhood classroom in a public school building, Lowell Johnson is taking great care to set up the evening's activities around a circus theme: an art table with paper strips, balloons, glue, and scissors for making paper chains and clown collars; clown make-up in the dress-up area; a stand-up cardboard clown, mouth open, a for pom-pom toss; a balance beam set out for "walk the high wire"; a mat for tumbling; circus books displayed in the book area; "barbells" set up for "be a strong person"; cup stilts; a Barbie and Ken, and He-Man collection to stimulate a discussion of gender. There are lots of non-circus activities too: a water area; a table full of puzzles; side-by-side easels.

At 6:30, 11 dads begin drifting in with their preschoolers. Two burly T-shirted men are in the dress-up area painting clown make-up on their sons. Another dad is helping his daughter with housekeeping and a Barbie doll, while six guys are absorbed in helping glue yarn-hair on top of balloons. One mom has come too and fits in easily while Lowell wanders through the room keeping an eye on everything.

Shortly after 7 p.m., when Lowell sounds a chime for clean-up time, dads sponge their kids off at the sink. Two teacher assistants come into the room and unobtrusively gather the children at tables for snack while the men drift out of the room and down the hall for their discussion group.

### Learning Together in the Group

After a few announcements—next week they will meet at the Children's Museum and the following week they're taking a trip to the Air Force airport where one of the fathers is in the reserves—Lowell begins easing the group into a discussion of doll play. "A week ago we started talking about Ken and Barbie. I wondered if anybody had any ideas or thoughts about that. Did any of the kids play with them tonight?"

"Since we had this discussion I was much more conscious of Julie playing with her dolls," says a dad in a Hardee's T-shirt. "I had seen it but never paid much attention to it, never got actively involved. This time I asked her questions about what she was thinking of, what was happening in her doll play."

"My kids ask me to play dolls with them,"

says a man in a striped shirt, "but I feel totally inadequate in the play room. I didn't do that as a child. I don't know how to play dolls. If I try to get involved it all ends. Maybe they sense my boredom. What do you do?"

"I observe," says the guy in the Badgers sweatshirt. "I try to take cues from her. I don't ask questions. That just kills it."

Lowell guides the discussion for a half-hour, 11 grown men trying to learn from one another—and from the one woman in the group, the designated "expert"—how to play dolls. None of this is didactic. There are no explicit lessons. But the men learn that it's not atypical for a dad to feel uncomfortable. They realize that their kids do different types of dramatic play with different dolls and that the types of dolls that are available—and the types of questions parents ask when kids are playing—make for a subtle but important type of education.

"The first time I even saw a black doll was here," says one dad, prompting the group to a discussion of which stores in the area carry black dolls and ways in which dolls can reinforce both racism and sexism.

"Initially, the hardest part for me with the dads was the discussion," says Lowell. "I was using a structured approach with the moms' groups—a presentation on a specific topic—but it didn't work with the men. Then I took courses on group dynamics and adult development and my discussions started to go better. I've used more of the group process techniques and tried to draw out topics from the dads."

Topics have ranged from dealing with prejudice, to how you feel when you come home from a long day at work and the kids don't want to have anything to do with you, to getting a vasectomy — and they seem to have an impact. After several discussions of discipline, one Nigerian father told the group that he had broken and thrown away his stick, the traditional instrument of discipline in his family.

The discussion isn't over, but it too has the seeds of a meaningful lesson as the men hear about the importance of doll play. They walk back down the hall to join their children thinking about one of Lowell's questions: "How does a boy learn to be a father if he's never had a chance to practice caretaking?"

## Circle Time

Back in the classroom, the men sit in a circle around tumbling mats with kids on their laps as Lowell announces the circus theme and assumes the role of ringmaster. All the kids pretend they are strong men and women breaking the paper chains, then go through a sequence of acrobatics, each child attempting a somersault or cartwheel on the mats in the middle. Next Lowell-the-Lion-Tamer holds up a hoop for each child-lion to jump through, with dads and kids roaring and clapping to each jump.

Following more games, it's time to calm down the wound-up children and prepare to go home. With children cradled on their parents' laps, Lowell leads the group through the non-sexist lyrics of 'Bumping Up and Down in My Little Red Wagon'—"Johnny will fix it with his hammer, Susie will fix it with her pliers," and then the closes with "Blackbird in the Sky": "Two little blackbirds sitting on a cloud, one named quiet, one named loud. Fly away quiet, fly away loud..." And with that it's time for all the blackbirds and their dads to go home—until next week.

## A Support Group for Men

But not all go home right away. Five of the guys—including a sales manager for Procter & Gamble, an elementary school counselor, and a maintenance engineer   take their kids to McDonald's for what has turned into a weekly ritual: dads dinner out with the kids.

For all of them, both Dad and Me and the trip to McDonald's has become a must-do event in their busy lives. "I've had several people working for me and they always ask about my calendar: 'What's JC?' It's Julie's Class. I have everything planned around it. Next week I have an appointment with the CEO of a major customer, and I've scheduled it for Thursday because on Tuesday we have Dad and Me."

"I do a lot of juggling to keep Tuesdays open," says Valdi. "I just say it's very sacred."

"Sometimes I'll have to fly in late from out of town," says Bill. "But I ask Valdi to take my daughter to the class and then I meet them there."

The only real problem with Dad and Me is that it ends after kindergarten. "Having been with her for three years, how do you replace this activity?" asks one dad. "Even if she gets involved with Girl Scouts or something, it's not the same. If they had a program for six-year-olds next year, we'd be there."

## Contact

Lowell Johnson, Parent Educator
White Bear Lake Area Schools
3559 White Bear Avenue
White Bear Lake, MN 55110
(612) 653-2715

## TIPS

- **Spend at least two weeks on ice breakers so the men will open up.** Physical activity—even throwing a ball of yarn around—helps.
- **Hear men out.** Find out what they're interested in, not what you think is important.
- **If you're a woman leading a group, let men know that you're the facilitator, not the expert.** And talk about your experiences with children just as they would—including the temper tantrums that happened in church.
- **Play down occupations when making introductions.** That will let men relate as father to father, without preconceived ideas or worries about their relative status.
- **Ask men "what do you think?" instead of "what do you feel?"** Thinking doesn't put them on the spot and eases them into sharing their feelings.

# CHAPTER
# 12
# The Monthly Men's Group

## FAIRFAX-SAN ANSELMO CHILDREN'S CENTER

**Location:** Fairfax, CA

**Services:** 125 children from 3 months to 10 years; 10 mildly handicapped

**Diversity:** 75% Caucasian, 10% Black, 10% Asian, 5% Hispanic

**Family Income:** 90% low or moderate

**Funding:** 60% State of California; 40% United Way and parent fees on sliding scale

*The monthly Saturday morning men's group is the centerpiece of more than a decade of including men in all facets of this program, which serves a low-and moderate-income population just north of San Francisco. Every classroom, from infant through school-age care, has a male teacher. Over 90 percent of fathers or male friends are involved with the center in one way or another, and almost 100 percent attend parent conferences, whether or not they are living at home. "Our goal is that all the men feel comfortable coming here," says associate director Stan Seiderman, "that they feel valued and that they feel they have as much stake in the center as their wives. It doesn't have to be exactly the same stake, but they should feel this is their center."*

### Background

It's hard to tell at first glance that this program is for families of modest means. Set in Marin, one of the wealthiest counties in the United States, it is housed in a facility most early childhood educators only dream of: a one-story former elementary school at the entrance to a magnificent tree-filled county park.

Since 1980, under the visionary direction of Ethel Seiderman, the center has been leading the Parent Services Project, a national training effort to shift the role of centers from child care to family care and to test the idea that expanded support to families can reduce parental stress and create healthier families. "Family support is the missing piece in child care," says Ethel Seiderman. "But once you get into it, the second missing piece is the involvement of men."

"We took at look at our application forms," says Stan Seiderman, "and realized that unless you're the father and living with the child, there's no place for you on the form. Since we did most of our intake with mothers, we didn't know a man was involved until he showed up to pick up the child. Then the staff wondered who he was and if they should give the child to him. And even if staff knew him, we saw how uncomfortable he felt as he sauntered in and out. If we had a parent-teacher conference, only mothers would show up. It was clear something was wrong. We saw the problem and took some action to change it."

Stan organized a small planning committee of men which sent a letter inviting "all men who are fathers in the program, either by biology, social role, or legal convention . . . to bring their children and join us for a hearty breakfast. . . . Also, and very important, in those families where there are no men-fathers, you may still send your child to this breakfast. For those children, the committee members will be their fathers (for the morning)."

The initial Men's Breakfast was held on Saturday, August 1, 1981, with 20 out of 80 fathers showing up to meet and suggest what the center could do to get men more involved. The natural vehicle was staring them in the face. "We hit on the Men's Breakfast because it fit," says Stan. Three hours on the weekend was doable. It gave men a chance to spend time with their kids, meet other guys, learn about the center and ways they could help it, and have a group discussion — guided by a highly skilled leader — about parenting. It allowed fathers who may not live with their child a place to spend time with their child. It also allowed boyfriends, uncles, grandfathers and Big Brothers to get involved.

The Men's Breakfast has continued on the first Saturday of every month since then, reaching at least 50 percent of all fathers, anywhere between 6 and 20 dads at a time. It has evolved to a format that includes breakfast, discussion, and doing fix-ups at the center—repairing playground equipment, painting, whatever needs to be done. And it has spawned an annual picnic and camping trip that includes almost all families associated with the program.

The breakfast has become a rite of initiation for fathers new to the center. "I wouldn't say I'm the champion of networking," says one man, "but it's a good way to meet other fathers."

Lawrence Reynolds has been a participant for 10 years with three children of wide age spans. "It's sort of a self-sustaining process. I don't need to be encouraged because I see the benefits and I appreciate the opportunity to meet other fathers. I get out of it that there are other men raising children and having the same problems. It's a safer situation for men to express themselves and not have to play macho roles. It makes me feel closer to the center, that I'm more than just a client."

## The Men's Breakfast

Shortly before 9 a.m. Stan Seiderman is scraping a skillet in the kitchen that looks onto a large room where breakfast tables are set up with cereal and grapefruit juice donated by the local Food Bank. He is tearing circles out of wheat bread, preparing to make the "hole in one" style egg that he learned as a boy from his aunt. Today he's going to teach dads how to get their kids to eat an egg.

The seven kids who have arrived with their dads do, in fact, eat the eggs. While they roam around pretending they are lions and tigers— under the supervision of a child care worker— the men talk over donuts and coffee. What could pass for chit-chat is actually a very instructive discussion of fathers' everyday worries about childrearing: How do you get your kids to sleep? Should you lie down with them or not? What should you do about a bee sting? It is all gently guided by the deep-voiced, roly-poly Stan, who always seems to have a smile on his face and a laugh around the corner, a guy who seems at ease with himself and everybody else.

After an hour of breakfast and discussion, with everybody feeling quite friendly, Stan asks for introductions, gives a history of the Men's Group (two of the dads are new to the center), and explains some of the supports it can offer. "This Christmas we'll look at toy catalogs and help guys pick toys and understand what's appropriate. We always want to know how the center is serving you, if it's meeting your needs."

Another hour passes in what seems like five minutes and Stan asks the men to gather their kids so all can help in fixing the center. A procession of dads and kids goes from room to room changing lights. The kids get lots of praise for "helping carry" (i.e., walking alongside) the heavy ladders their dads are holding, and the men are clearly pleased to be helping the center.

**During the monthly men's breakfast, the men eat, discuss needs, and even do repairs at the center.**

## TIPS

- **Examine your beliefs.** The first order of business is to consciously and deliberately determine that you do wish to relate to men, that there is something good that happens when you do.
- **Look at your internal practices**—such as interviewing and enrolling families or holding parent-teacher conferences—and see what barriers may be getting in the way of involving more men.
- **Offer men something to do that will make them feel welcome and useful.** If you're comfortable about asking, they'll accept quite easily.
- **Have men on the staff.** It makes it easier for men to feel identified.
- **Create something that is unique for men.** For men to come in, they need a sense of ownership separate and apart from being partners with women.
- **Make a special effort— but make sure it's a continuing effort.** The men's agenda needs attention and shouldn't be left to chance.

Is this stereotyping, casting men into traditional roles? "The men like doing this," says Ethel Seiderman. "We're not into tokenism or stereotypes here. A task requires know-how. A couple of men did the lighting for our Friday night basketball game and other activities. I'm not going to run in and say 'show me.' I say up front, 'I'm really smart, but I don't want to fix the lights.'"

### Special Events

Because not all men at the center could or wanted to attend the Men's Breakfast, the planning committee decided to try out a camping trip and later a picnic. Since excluding women seemed to fly in the face of the center's commitment to family support, the Men's Group now sponsors special annual events open to all. The camping trip draws virtually all of the Asian fathers, who are usually the most reluctant to attend the Men's Breakfast. And the picnic and barbecue at nearby Angel Island gives all the dads a chance to contribute and show off their skills to the family.

### A Father-Friendly Environment

But it's not just the Men's Breakfast or special events that make the center receptive to men. There are male teachers in every classroom as a matter of principle—educational principle, not quota filling—just as there have been men on staff ever since the center opened. "To make this place welcoming to men," says Ethel Seiderman, "you have to have men on the staff. It isn't a matter of affirmative action but of what kids need to grow healthy. Kids need both sexes in their lives. They need to see the range of what we bring to them. I can't remember a time when we haven't had men on staff."

Ethel Seiderman is also aware that men are more suspect in the child care environment, that the comfort level she has tried to create about

male staffing is atypical. "Some women won't leave men alone with kids. When we go on trips we have men and women going together, because a man is more vulnerable. But at the center, Gerald does our late care. The day I can't go home and leave Gerald alone here I'd go crazy. Our men change diapers and take kids being toilet trained to the bathroom."

It's also a matter of principle that so many photos in the Center's publications and on its walls show men with children. "It's because I want men to be more prominent," says Stan Seiderman. "This is a woman's type organization and if you allow it, it will become totally that. You have to work against that."

To raise consciousness further, Stan has created a regular feature for the center's monthly newsletter. "Stan's Corner" presents his male perspective on life at the center and also offers a regular slot for male staff or parents to contribute. He's also developed a slide show about the center's efforts to include men which he uses as a training tool for the national Parent Services Project. "It demonstrates some of the variety that's available to children where there are men around.

To make sure that men attend parent-teacher meetings—and virtually 100 percent do—the center makes special efforts to reach men living outside the home. It has developed a special "men's list," an unofficial addition to the official government-reportable figures. Making it a point to include men sometimes leads to tension between mothers and fathers. According to Ethel Seiderman, "There's no doubt you'll get into a conference where the emotions are so high that you have to set them aside and say, 'let's get back to what we're focused on here— your child.'"

More than a decade's work at involving men has transformed the atmosphere at the Fairfax-Anselmo Children's Center. "The men feel very comfortable," says Stan. "This is as much their place as the women's. They have no problem talking to staff, sitting around chatting, stopping by the office, doing the things they never did before. Staff feel very comfortable with them. They're not strangers in the life of the child. They're not treated like some guy who's delivering milk."

### Contact

Stan Seiderman
Associate Director
Fairfax-San Anselmo Children's Center
199 Porteous Avenue
Fairfax, CA 94901
(415) 454-1811

**Children help the men repair things around the center, including cleaning the center's van.**

## CHAPTER
### ⑬
# Fathers Working Together

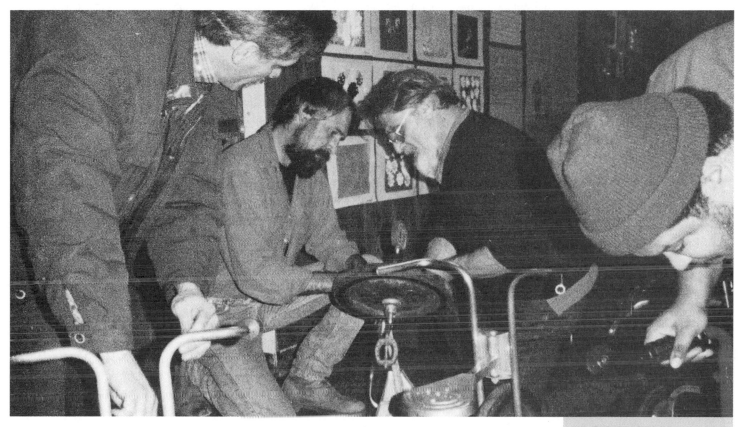

*T*his public school-based early childhood program celebrated its 25th anniversary in 1990 and used the occasion to rename the center the Florence S. Brown New York State Pre-Kindergarten Program. Ms. Brown had been the center's project supervisor for 20 years before she passed away. In the closing days before she died, she said :"Don't let the fathers' program die after I'm gone." Administrators who have followed Ms. Brown have kept her legacy alive. The program has an active Fathers' Group, promotes male involvement from intake onward, and offers a welcoming environment and activities to encourage men's participation throughout the year.

### Background

For many years, this program operated out of an elementary school building in a low-income area of Rochester and held weekly meetings open to all parents and family members. But in 1986, three fathers and a grandfather requested that a "Fathers' Group" be formed so they could discuss issues more closely related to men as parents. Over a year's time, the group grew to 14 active participants — fathers or other significant males who repaired broken toys, painted the children's large activity room, purchased materials and built an outdoor sandbox for the playground. Working with Florence Brown and her staff, the group then planned the first Pre-K Father and Child Night — a huge success that brought many men out to share classroom activities with their children.

Soon even more men began to attend regular meetings, including several who were unemployed due to a downturn in the local economy. What started as a core group of four has grown to as many as 25 men being involved in one form or another.

### A Place to Congregate

Most of the 30 parents who attend the weekly meeting held for each half-day session are women. But a significant number of men also show up to join the discussion led by an outside

**FLORENCE S. BROWN PRE-K CENTER**

**Location:** Rochester, N.Y.

**Serves:** 256 3- and 4- year-olds in half-day sessions

**Diversity:** 63% African-American, 26% Caucasian, 9% Hispanic, 2% Asian-American

**Family Income:** 80% low, 20% middle to high

**Funding:** 80% New York State Department of Education; 20% local school district

speaker. Mike, who works the night shift, comes because :"I get a sense of community from this group. I also learn a lot from the other people who have similar problems with their kids." Joe, who has a child with special needs, says :"I've learned that each of my kids is a unique individual. Each one has his own special needs."

When there are no meetings being held, the large open meeting room is set aside for parents. There's always coffee, a bulletin board announcing upcoming events, and a chance to sit and talk — all in keeping with Ms. Brown's philosophy that "Parents are the most important people."

### Finding and Welcoming Men

Staff work consistently to make sure those important people include men. At intake, the parent coordinator attempts to determine if a single mother-headed household has a male available. Staff greet both mothers and fathers warmly when they bring their children into the center. A recent flyer written in both Spanish and English is typical of the program's outreach: "Pre-K Fathers: Come to a meeting for lunch, fun, to learn and to plan." And the original Father and Child Night now occurs both in the fall and the spring, welcoming men to follow the child's daily schedule.

### The Fathers' Group

Although fathers attend the regular parent meetings, they also have their own group which meets once a month at lunchtime and once a month in the evening. Discussions are led by either Gerald Daniels, a father of four, who has had three children enrolled in the center, or by another volunteer. Sometimes outside speakers are brought in to lead discussions of topics such

as "conflict resolution" and "how to talk to your child about sex." One former member, Reverend Lynn Turner, an ordained minister and engineer who now works for the Rochester Urban League, still contributes even though his twins graduated from Pre-K five years ago.

Members of the fathers' group are active both practically and politically. Recently the group built a sandbox, and one dad does weekly maintenance of the tricycles. When the Rochester school district talked about cutting the three-year-old program out of the Pre-K budget, Daniels and eight group members lobbied the superintendent of schools. A scheduled half-hour meeting ran for two hours; the fathers emerged with a promise that funds would be found to keep three-year-olds in Pre-K.

As much as it serves the program, the fathers' group benefits its members even more. Prezel's daughter came home in tears one day saying "My friends don't think I have a daddy," because his long hours of work meant he was never around. Through the group, Prezel has been learning how to stay connected to his children—and that he isn't the only man having such problems. According to James, "The group has helped me to get in touch with my emotions. I have gained a better understanding of my child when I learn what she is doing, and I have learned to grow along with her."

### Contact

Hilda L. Ortiz, Project Supervisor
Janet McElrath, Parent Group Leader
500 Webster Ave.
Rochester, NY 14609
(716) 288-2410

**Fathers gain a better understanding of their children when they learn about what they are doing.**

## CHAPTER

# Recruiting Men

*T*  *hrough its Manpower program, this Ohio Head Start program recruits men from area churches, businesses and other professions to volunteer in classrooms where they become important role models for young children. Men and women become part of the Head Start extended family by attending weekly two-hour literacy sessions. Males are encouraged to become part of the agency's policy council, and there is an active attempt to hire men as teachers, social-service and other program staff. Almost nine percent of the staff—18 out of 206—are men.*

### Background

"No one woke up one day and said 'we need more men in the program,'" says president and CEO Marilyn E. Thomas, who was educational coordinator before becoming the

head of the organization in 1977. "There has always been an emphasis on parent involvement. At a certain point, we realized we needed to include fathers too!"

Since the mid-80s, Mrs. Thomas has worked with her two vice presidents (one male, one female) and parent involvement coordinator, Jeanette Taylor, to get more men involved. Their unified sense of the importance of the male role in Head Start, the continuity of their effort, and their "push from the top" has helped bring males into the program as paid staff. Having a man in a high level, visible position hasn't hurt either. "Some may think this is sexist," says vice president Jerry Scott, "but I'm sometimes the one who is chosen to have a 'man-to-man' talk with one of the male staff members."

Beyond being positive and supportive, the

---

**MIAMI VALLEY CHILD DEVELOPMENT CENTERS**

**Location:** Dayton, OH

**Service:** 1,968 children in 35 centers

**Diversity:** 60% African-American, 40% Caucasian

**Family Income:** Head Start eligibility

**Funding:** $4 million annually through Head Start and local agencies

**It takes real commitment to recruit more men as staff and volunteers.**

program administrators have taken definite steps to bring more men into the program both as staff and as volunteers.

## Male Staff

The program has tried hard, in spite of the limitation of low salaries, to lure men into paid staff positions. A certified teacher with a bachelor's degree who works in Head Start makes $11,000 a year; a public-school teacher with the same credentials starts out with an $18,000 annual salary.

"We take about ten extra steps to get and keep men in the program, but it's difficult," says Thomas, "especially if they're the single wage earner in the household." Those steps have yielded a staff that is nine percent male, compared to the 1989 national average of five percent of men employed in child care. The staff of 206 includes 18 men: six teachers and teacher assistants, four social workers, three custodians, one food service distributor, three bus drivers, and one staff vice president.

The program recruits males by local newspaper advertising, announcements in placement offices in local colleges, and flyers on bulletin boards in local school districts, health facilities, and local businesses. It also relies on word of mouth—spread by parents and staff—to let men know that Head Start welcomes their participation.

## Male Volunteers

Project Manpower was initiated by vice president Betty Toney in 1989. She got the idea one day when Dayton's mayor, Clay Dixon, was invited to visit a Head Start classroom to talk to the children.

"Do you know who's responsible for bringing water to your house?" the mayor asked a group of awed and attentive 3-and 4-year-olds. The children weren't really sure what mayors did, but Dixon went on to explain that he was responsible for water, garbage collection and a host of other public services. Inspired by the mayor's visit, Toney was sure that bringing significant male figures into the classroom would be good for the children. If National Cash Register could release executives to take part in the United Way of Ohio, why couldn't they release some employees to volunteer in Head Start?

Toney created a flyer for professional, church, and business groups suggesting some of the many things that a man could do in Head Start classrooms: reading a story, assisting kids with computer operations, or just talking about his work or hobby. The Young Democrats League was the first to respond, followed by Concerned Christian Men. Now Toney has a roster of over 25 professionals who have signed up to volunteer their time, including bankers, lawyers and others. Habeeb Shafeek, a former counselor with the Dayton Urban League who has volunteered in the classroom says, "This has allowed me to work with youngsters—to get me involved in the lives of kids before they became at risk." A single, male parent—though ineligible for Head Start—Shafeek was so impressed with what he saw in the classrooms that he went on to hold a number of policy-making positions in the local and national Head Start program.

## Male Policy Council Members

In May 1991, there were four men on the sixteen-member Policy Council. To achieve this relatively high percentage, the parent involvement coordinator and the 22 family services workers—four of whom were men—visit parent meetings at all 35 centers to talk about parent involvement and to encourage male involvement. They make sure that at least one of the male policy council members comes to the local meeting to send a strong signal that the meetings are for men and women. According to Jeanette Taylor, "You can talk about male involvement, but men need to see other men to be convinced that they have a place in the program."

The family service workers identify and encourage men who may have leadership qualities. Roger, one of the family service workers, thinks it is especially important for him to be in Head Start for the young fathers: "Many of these young men don't know how to be fathers. I can relate to them on a man-to-man basis." Roger also sees the need to be there for the children, many of whom come from single-parent (mother) homes.

Raymond, a father of seven children, got involved when his wife suggested that he "take a look" at the program his children were attending. When he saw the growth his daughters were experiencing, this former high school football star (called Big Mac by his admirers), who now works for the juvenile court system, ran for membership on the Policy Council. Because he likes to make known his wishes for the program, he quickly rose to vice president.

David, a PC member with eight children, first felt "outnumbered by the women" when he came to spend time in the center. But a family service worker suggested that he might feel comfortable on the Policy Council, and he now enjoys the feeling of being able to influence the program for his children. John, who works in manufacturing on an evening shift, lost a run for the presidency of his local parent body, but is now able to attend the Policy Council, meetings that are held during the day. He feels Head Start has helped him to feel greater self-esteem as a black male. "If a dad is needed in Head Start, I'm going to be that dad!"

### Project Enrich

Part of the funding from a $40,000 Dayton United Way "Project Enrich" grant provides stipends for literacy training that could lead to the completion of the G.E.D. Here too, the program has been modestly successful at luring men into Head Start. In the 1990 school year, five of the 56 participants were men.

Collie, a Head Start grandfather, receives $10 for each of the literacy events he attends, ranging from a two-hour workshop on "From Preschool to Kindergarten" to a trip to the local Afro-American Museum. The program has been inventive with its offerings, going beyond classroom lectures. It showed parents how to use the local library, where they emerged with library cards. It had a parent tour of a supermarket, led by a nutritionist who explained the value of purchasing fresh vegetables as opposed to canned vegetables; groups study the stories in the local newspaper and then tour the newspaper office to see how the paper was created.

Patricia Peroutka, vice president of finance, thinks the stipends can be a good idea, but complains that they can be "a pain in the neck" because of the paperwork requirements related to disbursement. When the program first began, parents who were receiving public assistance reported the extra income from the stipends, raising questions from local authorities about the impact of extra income on a family's grant. Since that time, parents are reminded that stipends are reimbursement for travel, food, and babysitting costs and are not considered income. Vice president Betty Toney is a staunch supporter of the stipends. "First you have to get the parent's attention—the stipend will do that. Once in, you have to keep their attention with strong programming. Then they will stick around even when the stipend is not available."

### Contact

Marilyn E. Thomas, President and CEO
Jeanette Taylor, Parent Involvement Coordinator
1034 Superior Ave.
Dayton, Ohio 45407-1900
Tel: (513) 278-8293
Fax: (513) 276-8097

**Welcome men's creative participation in your program.**

**TIPS**

• **Encourage mothers to communicate** the program's interest in the involvement of men. Women are often the first contact when new families are enrolled.

• **Encourage men and women who are together in the family to alternate schedules** for picking up children or volunteering in the classroom.

• **Ask! It is important for center staff to ask parents to help.** We need you! is the message that should be constantly sent through words and actions.

• **Be positive. Be patient. Be adaptable.** If one strategy doesn't work, try another.

## CHAPTER

# Male Involvement Specialists

**THE OUNCE OF PREVENTION FUND**

**Location:** Chicago, IL.

**Services:** nine Head Start centers with double sessions, serving 1,100 preschoolers

**Diversity:** 60% African-American, 20% Hispanic, 15% Caucasian, 5% Asian

**Family Income:** 95% below poverty guidelines

**Funding:** $2.25 million annually

*A*t three of its Head Start Centers, the Ounce-of-Prevention fund employs part-time male involvement specialists, men from the local communities who actively recruit fathers and other male relatives. Working both inside and outside of the classroom, the specialists serve as classroom assistants, trip chaperones, meeting facilitators for fathers and other males, and recruiters of male high school student volunteers.

### Background

In October 1990, there were no men on the staff, and involvement by fathers or other men was almost nonexistent. That's when Jean Murphy, director of Early Childhood Services, introduced a plan to hire and train parents or other Head Start relatives as male involvement specialists. The program is now funded through the Career Paths for Parents Program, providing adults with

an entry to the world of work, and children with a significant male presence in their lives.

Supervisor Lisa Russell oversees a three-phase program open to high school graduates: orientation and training, on the job training, and job-readiness counseling leading to further employment. Between September and June the male involvement specialists work a 20-hour week and receive a cash stipend.

"My weekly duties vary as I am needed," says Michael Poe of the Children's Home Aid Society of Illinois, "but generally on Mondays I work in the classroom, helping the kids learn their shapes, colors, etc. I read stories. I do whatever the teachers need me to do. One day I dressed up as a fireman in the classroom. The kids love to play dress-up and they really enjoyed seeing me dress up. On Tuesdays, I usually do outdoor male recruitment. I greet men who are dropping their kids off and picking them up from the center. I let them know what's going on in the center, keep them up to date. At first, some of them thought I was gay, because they don't really think a man's place is working with little kids. But because I talk to them man-to-man, and let them see me out in the community, playing ball and hanging out, that makes them feel better about me as a man working in daycare. They accept me and want to know what's happening in the center. Some of them want to know what they can do."

Larry Stribling, the Male Involvement Specialist at the Garfield Head Start Center, says "I am the kids' role model. I play games, tie shoes, help kids learn to write their names, help them to learn good from bad. During a typical week, I do paperwork, observe kids in the classroom, assist the teachers in the classroom. I do what is needed to be done wherever, whenever. Sometimes I am a food aide, helping to get the lunch or snacks ready. The cook at the Garfield Center is a man, so when I help out in the kitchen, the kids get to see two men in the kitchen. Sometimes I help the custodian with the cleaning. Usually, I give the boys handshakes and the girls hugs, but sometimes the boys need hugs too."

"I rotate from class to class in order to spend time with all of the children," says Vernon Smith of the St. Paul Head Start Center: "The boys especially need to connect with a positive male image. For these little boys, I am that male image. You could say that's my job, that's what I do every day. My schedule is flexible so it varies from week to week. I also attend training sessions outside the center."

## Contact

Lisa Russell
Coordinator of Male Involvement Program
188 Randolph Street
Chicago, IL
(312) 853-6080

**TIPS**

• **Train your Head Start staff to be receptive to male involvement.** Make them aware of the benefits of male involvement for the center and for the children.
• **Add the male involvement specialist position to your Head Start staff.** Make a specific effort to have men in your program through direct hiring or by using parent training funds.
• **Have a specific place where men can feel comfortable in your center.** If space is a problem, allocate "males only" meeting times for your parents' room.
• **Make it clear** to both mothers and staff that male involvement has not become a priority to the exclusion of mother involvement.

**Lisa Russell works with male involvement specialists, who recruit family members for the program.**

## CHAPTER
## 16
# Reaching Fathers at Home

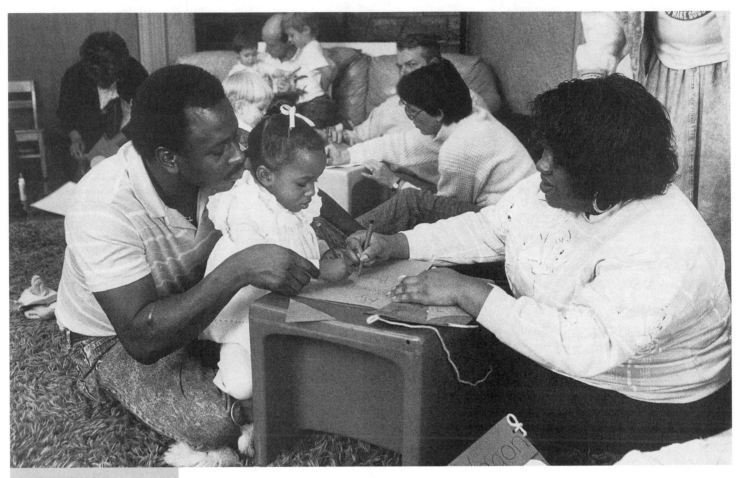

## PARENTS AS TEACHERS

**Location:** St. Louis, MO.

**Services:** 85,000 families statewide

**Diversity:** varies from community to community

**Funding:** approximately $570/family depending on the agency

*Widely recognized as a national model, Parents as Teachers advocates that parents are children's first teachers. In order to give all children the best possible start from birth, PAT provides regular home visits and group meetings to educate parents— regardless of income—on their growing and developing child. The program makes a strong effort to include fathers and not just mothers as first teachers.*

### Background

In 1981 the Missouri Department of Elementary and Secondary Education launched Parents as Teachers as a pilot project to help parents educate themselves about the physical and mental development of children from infancy to 3 years, and how they could act as advocates and first teachers for their children. Since then the program has expanded steadily. In 1985 an education act expanded the program statewide to every school district, making services available to 10 percent of families in the state; in 1986 funds were appropriated for 20 percent of families; in 1987 funds were made available for the parents of three- and-four-year-olds. By 1990, 110,000 families were served statewide and screening for developmental disabilities was provided for more than 55,000 children under 3 years. PAT's goal by the year 2,000 is to make services available to all families. The number of PAT programs in Missouri and across the nation has now passed the 1,000 mark.

Parents learn about PAT in a variety of ways. Some view "Born to Learn," a six-minute videotape underwritten by Sears Portrait Studios that is shown to expectant and new parents in prenatal clinics and hospitals throughout the state. Some learn from other parents and friends who have participated in the program, or are referred from social service, health, and other agencies.

## Program Features

PAT provides home visits every four to six weeks by a parent educator trained in child development. (They may be scheduled weekly or biweekly when the family situation warrants it.) Home visits help parents develop their skills in observing and interacting with children, and give them a chance to ask questions about their child's growth and development. Group parent meetings give them opportunities to share child rearing experiences with other parents and discuss topics of concern, such as toilet training, discipline, and sibling rivalry. Parents also get to engage with their children in supervised music and arts and craft activities.

Parent educators try to schedule home visits when both parents are available. When that is not possible notes are left for the father asking him to call or to leave a note with his concerns and questions. When fathers are present during the home visit the parent educator has activities for both parents to do and asks for their opinions and observations about the child's behavior and development. Parent educators also suggest activities specifically for dads such as games to exercise motor skills or making Mother's Day gifts with the child.

Group activities are also regularly scheduled for parents and children. The most popular for fathers, offered during both spring and fall, is the Messy Activities Evening on the playground or indoors at the school. Primarily for parents and children over age 2, it includes activities such as painting with water and with balls, a water table, collage making, sand box, swings, and sliding boards.

In May 1991, Messy Activities in the Ferguson-Florissant School District drew some 33 mothers, 28 fathers, and 70 children including some older siblings of children enrolled in the program. Most fathers were very appreciative that the Messy Activities night was a regularly scheduled event because it gave them an opportunity to play with their kids. One dad commented, "I wish the Messy Activities were scheduled more often, maybe once a month. Usually when I leave home, Jeremy is sleeping and when I come back I'm beat and too tired to play with him, so I really miss a great deal of his growing and changing, and I would love it if I knew that there would be a special night to spend time playing with him."

Messy Activities aside, fathers seem to find PAT valuable as a source of information for understanding what behaviors are age-appropriate for their children. Mike Massato relates,

"Parents as Teachers has helped me to know what to expect from my kid, and when. I never knew that before."

## Teen Parents

In 1987, Parents as Teachers instituted a program for teen parents and parents-to-be enrolled at the Ferguson-Florissant High School; by spring of 1991 there were 200 young women and 40 young men enrolled for individual and group counseling and for home visits to assess the development of their children up to three years.

In addition to monthly co-ed meetings, the program holds sessions for "Moms Only" and "Dads Only." Teen fathers relate that the program has been instructive and informative for them on many levels. As one young man with a three-year-old daughter says, "The program has helped me to grow up. I had to learn to cope with a lot of things—my daughter, her mother and her grandmother. That's really hard. Everybody wants something from me—money, attention, something. The program helps me know what my rights are, as well as my responsibilities. Until I started coming to these meetings I didn't know that I had any rights."

## Contact

Mildred Winter, Executive Director
Parents as Teachers National Center, Inc.
9374 Olive Boulevard
St. Louis, MO 63132
Telephone: (314) 432-4330

While attending a Parents as Teachers group meeting, a father helps his son with fine-motor skills.

CHAPTER

# Bus Drivers As Recruiters

## PARENTS IN COMMUNITY ACTION

**Location:** Minneapolis, MN.

**Services:** 2,000 preschoolers; waiting list of 1,000

**Diversity:** 53% African-American, 20% Caucasian, 14% Asian, 10% Native American, 3% Hispanic

**Funding:** $8 million annual budget

*R*edefining the role of the bus driver is one of several ingenious keys to male involvement at PICA, which operates the Head Start program in Hennepin County, Minnesota. Drivers, most of whom are male, spend an hour a day in the classroom and attend all educational staff meetings. They also recruit men from the community as volunteer bus riders, which leads to their participation in PICA's Parent Training Project. These and other programs, along with an active commitment to involving men in every facet of the program, have produced results: Almost 40 percent of parents showing up at PICA events are men.

### Background

PICA was founded in 1969 to operate the Head Start program in Hennepin County and ensure that parents have the opportunity to become involved in all the program's facets. Since then it has lived up to its name and to that pledge. Sixty-seven percent of its board of directors, 73 percent of program administrators, and 49 percent of staff are current or former Head Start parents; 45 percent of staff are former welfare recipients; and 65 percent of staff are people of color.

PICA's 54 bus drivers are one of the keys to recruiting fathers and father figures at PICA. But that's because PICA has redefined the role of the bus driver to make him (or her) a full member of the educational team. Drivers spend at least an hour a day in the classroom, go on all field trips, and attend all parent-teacher conferences, monthly meetings of the Parent Activity Committee Council, and special events.

"Our transportation component is an integral part of our program," says executive director Alyce Dillon. "Other programs see it as divorced from families and children themselves. But drivers may be the only ones who are having day-to-day contact with a family, sometimes even more than the family services staff. I think our bus drivers realize how important they are."

With their knowledge of the program and of the community, PICA's drivers are in an ideal position to recruit the "parent volunteer rider" that every bus is required to have. At one time or another, half of PICA's parents have ridden the bus, and almost 30 percent of those volunteers are males.

In effect, PICA's bus drivers are its emissaries to the community, their presence and pride advertising the value of male involvement. "I love working with the children," says Jerry Hoskins, a driver who got involved with PICA over nine years ago, when he was unemployed and his son was in the program. "I have the gift of gab with parents, letting them know what's going on. We're involved in all program activities, including going with teachers on home visits. Out in the community, children see you and say, 'That's my bus driver!' The men who ride with me try to get more involved in the whole program. I think it's because they think, 'They're recognizing me too, and this is kind of fun. I don't have to do it everyday, but I'll help out when I can.'"

Interestingly and importantly, the transformation of the bus driver role at PICA was not as intentional as it might sound. What changed the position was making it an eight-hours-a-day rather than a six-hours-a-day job. "Thirty hours a week wasn't enough for people to survive on," says Alyce Dillon. "I personally felt we had to give people decent jobs and wages. This has as much to do with the evolution of our organization as anything. When we get better at one thing, it has a spillover effect on the other parts of the agency. One year we said we're going to get this transportation component together, and that then impacted the program. Everything overlaps everything else.

"It's like throwing a pebble into a pond, making the waves spread out."

## Parent Training Project

Another key to male involvement has been PICA's parent training project, which began as a pilot program in 1980. The goal was to teach parents about child development—and about what went on in their child's program—by having them work in a classroom other than their child's for over a six-week period.

What started as a pilot program with six parents getting an orientation has grown into a four-cycles-a-year program involving all classrooms and about 100 parents. And although it took three years for the first man to apply—an older Native American father who worked in a classroom with many Asian children and helped them to use more English—now more than 10 percent of all parent-trainees are men.

The story of David Buckney, a single parent with custody of his two preschool children, shows how the different parts of PICA link together. When the bus driver asked David to volunteer on the bus, helping kids on and off, he agreed. When the driver told him about PAC meetings, he got curious about the whole program. At his first PAC meeting he learned about the parent training program and applied. "At the time I just thought it was something to keep me occupied. I wasn't thinking it would lead to a job. But the more I did my training, the more I liked what I was doing. Just before you finish, they give you an application for substitute teaching. I substituted for a couple of months and then got a job."

Now an assistant teacher, David is taking community college courses in child development and moving into CDA training with the aspiration of becoming a head teacher. And he feels much more

**This parent works in his new role as teacher to make a difference to children.**

**Working with children as their teachers builds new confidence and understanding for parents.**

confident about raising his own children. "Parent training showed me how to see the child's point of view. I can understand three-, four-, and five-year old children better than if I wasn't involved."

### Special Events

PICA took a more active approach to reaching men in the early 1980s when it held its first parent breakfast. It started when Alyce Dillon heard about a Fathers and Kids breakfast at a Chicago program — "just when we were thinking about how to get men involved."

Women staff started the event, but as more men became part of the staff, it became a male event. According to Mary Bock, director of planning and development, "When male staff took over the special events, the men who came would see other men as important in this agency, running major events and doing good things for their kids. It's kind of a role modeling thing. There are a lot of strong women who run this program and it's important for them to know that the men can do an event."

School liaison director Gretchen Hengemuhle was surprised to see that the men were more open to talking with someone they didn't know. "I saw people exchanging phone numbers and saying, 'Hey man, we need to get together.'"

In addition to the Pancake Breakfast, which is now an annual event, PICA holds a Male-

Child Dinner in the spring, with a band, door prizes, and a variety of activities for parents and children to do together. In April 1991, 160 men turned out, plus 43 male staff, and 250 kids. "It was hard to tell who was staff and who was a visitor," says staff psychologist Dr. Norman Silberberg. "The men were working the food line, not the women, and most men focused on the kids."

Dr. Silberberg has offered special events for men to talk about parenting issues. Almost 100 men showed up for a discussion of discipline. "We talked about the concept of father as 'hit man,' that men shouldn't allow themselves to get into that position. It's self-defeating, because then men don't know how to relate to kids except as disciplinarians."

### Reaching the Man in the House

Rather than assuming men are unavailable, PICA staff assume that they can be made available, even if it takes a little work.

"The number one thing," says family advocate Shirley Morgan, especially for the women who have the boyfriend or husband in the home, is to let them know right up front that everything is confidential, that we want the men involved, as well as the mothers, and that we're not going to take their business into the street.

"If I know there's a father but he's not in the

home, I'll ask the mom right up front, 'Is it OK to call him or would you like to?' Even if she hasn't put his name down, I bring it up and see what happens. If she hems and haws, I ask if she'd like extra forms that she can send to him.

"There's lots of phone calling for every function we do. 'Do you need a ride? Do you plan to attend? It's OK for your boyfriend to be there.' For our Male-Child dinner we called everybody and said, 'You can send your child with anybody. It doesn't have to be the father.'"

Because so many families are headed by single mothers, PICA is particularly thoughtful about not having the presence of some fathers become a source of hurt or disappointment for children whose fathers do not live at home. "I don't think you can ignore the fact that other children say they don't have a dad," says Gretchen Hengemuhle. "We respond that some dads don't live at home, but everybody has a daddy. In our parent training programs, we remind kids that they have to share their parents with other kids. And when a child raises the question of the "other man" in the house, I ask, 'Will he come? Do you want him to come?' Then we talk with the mother."

### Hiring Men

Of PICA's staff of 250, 60 are men, distributed in all program areas: nutrition, teaching, advocacy, administration, and maintenance—with the heaviest concentration in transportation.

Alyce Dillon has always had a commitment to hiring from the community and to hiring men, but her thinking—and that of her staff—has evolved over the years. "It's always been important that men be involved. We believe that there should be a distribution of males and females available to young children as positive role models."

However, in the beginning PICA hired some men who didn't have the right skills or interests in young children; two of them ended up working for the railroad. And it also had resistance from several of its female teachers. School liaison Gretchen Hengemuhle says, "When I became a head teacher I said, 'Just don't give me a man.' I was an assistant teacher under two men, and it was a horrible experience."

"The reason it works better here now," says Dillon, "is the same reason our female staff works better. We've grown and evolved as an organization. We've become more competent, more proficient in looking at people's skills, seeing if they would fit within this organization or not. I don't think it has much to do with men or women. We've learned to trust our instincts. That's led us to hire men from the community who might not have a background working with children."

But that doesn't mean PICA hires men as tokens. According to Dillon, "A lot of the men who now work here approached me and said, 'Alyce, I need a job.' I said, 'Don't come over until you're serious about having a job, really ready. We're very serious about the work we do with young children. Don't come and screw it up.' I don't do the hiring directly, but I think they believe me, because they're ready when they come."

One of those is Brian Davis. "Alyce knew me from growing up," he says. "She took a chance on me. She knew I needed work and would do the best I could in whatever situation she put me into. I came into teaching as a sub; there was another man and he helped me, and I was trained by many different women in the organization. I could sense at times that some of the female teachers didn't know what kind of instructions to give me, and I'd have to take the initiative."

Now Brian has been working in the classroom for over five years and is training other men from the community. "I know a lot of them from growing up, and they're curious about what I'm doing. This year I had two of them in my classroom in the parent training program. When some of the men come in to volunteer they relay the message to others in the community that it's not just a woman's thing."

Alyce Dillon's convictions about hiring men have deepened. "In the last few years I've gotten more in touch with the political ramifications and the myths pervasive in our society about men, especially men of color: that they are absent from their children, that they don't care about their children. Most parents care about their children. Even people who do negative things in their lives still care for their kids and want something better for them. Involving these men in Head Start and hiring them became something not just for the children, but for the community. Unless you include the whole community you're not going to have a long-term impact."

### Contact

Bryan Nelson, Director of Health Services
Parents in Community Action
700 Humboldt Avenue N.
Minneapolis, MN 55411
(612) 377-7422

---

**TIPS**

• **Make parent involvement a core value.** Work at it every day. Male visibility helps.
• **Clearly state your position on male involvement.** Go on record that you want men involved.
• **Reach out to men every day of the year,** not just for special events.
• **Create a network of peers where familiarity can work for you.** It's not strangers asking strangers. It's friends asking friends, peers asking peers.

CHAPTER

# Reaching Men From the Community

## PINEBELT ASSOCIATION FOR COMMUNITY ENHANCEMENT

**Location:** Hattiesburg, MS.

**Service:** two Head Start centers for 466 children

**Diversity:** predominantly African-American

**Family Income:** poverty level

**Funding:** $1.3 million annually

*T*he Positive Male Role Program at PACE enlists men from businesses, churches, community organizations, and the local military base as classroom volunteers. On a regular basis 20 local men now act as teacher assistants in the classrooms; they serve as escorts for outings, help serve lunch, prepare snacks, put out cots in preparation for nap time, and have started a woodworking curriculum.

*Interestingly, none of these men are fathers of children enrolled in the program.*

### Background

Most of the parents at PACE Head Start are poor young women working in low-paying industries — poultry cleaning, sewing factories, and textile mills. Their jobs are very time consuming, often requiring 12-hour shifts, and leave little time for children and their needs. If there is a man in the household, it is usually not the father: of 466 families enrolled, only 75 have the natural father living at home.

The scarcity of men in the lives of PACE

children and the problems facing young black males in Mississippi — drug addiction, legal entanglements, and low-paying work if any — prompted parent involvement coordinator Gaye Newsome and executive director Peggy Butler to initiate a program that would provide positive contacts with men.

In 1989, Newsome wrote to and visited local churches and other organizations to solicit male volunteers for the Positive Male Role Program. Dr. Jawanza Kurijufu, a Chicago-based lecturer, was brought in to address parents and community residents on the perils of being black and male in American society.

Reaching out to the community was natural for PACE. In the previous 10 years, it had implemented a variety of volunteer programs including: Adopt-A-Center, where eight local associations, businesses, and churches provided some form of aid to the centers; Angel Tree, which provides food, clothing, and toys for families at Christmas; Dentist Adopt-a-Family, which provides preventive care for approximately two-dozen families; and an Alumni Association where Head Start students from as far back as 1965 host an annual teacher appreciation luncheon and work in classrooms.

To get a pool of volunteers for the Positive Male Role Model project, Newsome appealed to churches, men's associations, sympathetic businesses, and other organizations that didn't have to be convinced of its merits. Men who offered their time tended to be 10 to 20 years older than the natural fathers of the Head Start children, financially better off, and more community oriented, sharing the middle class values of the center's staff.

Today more than 25 local men are involved in classroom activities and outings. While the program is designed specifically to expose boys to positive male role models, girls are not excluded; the goal is to foster self-esteem in young children. All of the volunteers are also members of the local community, therefore available to parents for advice and casual communication. Each volunteer feels that he is in a partnership with Head Start or, as Peggy Butler puts it, "a partnership that is working towards saving children."

### Keeping the Commitment

It took a year to ensure that volunteers followed through, a year of getting to know the children well enough so that conflicts with work would yield to the commitment to the center.

Two of the most active volunteers are James Fluker, a Hess Oil employee who volunteers at Grace Love Center at least three days a week, and Reverend Johnson, a Seventh Day Adventist minister who volunteers one or two days per week. Recruited through his church, Mr. Fluker works the 11 p.m. to 7 a.m. shift, then comes to the center from 8 a.m. until 1 p.m. "I do whatev-

er the teacher is working on," he says, "play with shapes, blocks, painting. I help serve lunch, put the cots out for nap time, help put snacks out, take the boys to the bathroom, and get the kids ready to get on the bus. Sometimes I leave at one o'clock, but often I stay until the kids go home."

Reverend Johnson, who grew up without a father, feels he understands what that means for a young boy. He teaches tennis to the four-year-olds, reads stories, helps serve lunch, and bakes cookies for the children on holidays. "I help out as much as they let me," he says. "This program helps me to share some of my ideas about parenting. The program has helped me to appreciate the way my own kids have turned out. It makes my heart bleed to think about some of these youngsters. Like anyone else, I'm limited; there is only a certain amount that I can do to make the situation better."

### Contact

Peggy Butler, Director
710 Katie Avenue
Hattiesburg, MS 39401
Telephone: (601) 545-8110

**TIPS**

• **Be persistent and patient.** Don't be discouraged because one tactic doesn't work. You have to keep trying new things until you find something that works for your center and your families.

• **Don't limit yourself to parents.** Go to your community, to local churches and other male groups, and let them know that you need their help. You may be pleasantly surprised.

• **Tap the interests of your male volunteers.** We learned that some of them liked carpentry so we got some tools and started a woodworking project.

• **Use your staff to generate new ideas** and new ways to get and keep men in your program. Once some of our female teachers volunteered their husbands and brothers for a male class activity day. It was a great success!

Volunteers participate in classroom activities with the children.

One father's project was a family picnic, where the fathers cooked and served food.

CHAPTER
**19**

# The Men's Group

## ST. BERNADINE'S HEAD START

**Location:** Baltimore, MD

**Services:** 200 preschoolers

**Diversity:** 90% African-American

**Family Income:** poverty level

*D*on't Try to Handle It Alone, *reads a flyer advertising the weekly Men's Group at St. Bernardine's Head Start, located just a few blocks from street corners where men hang out all day with bottles of wine and at least one 11-year-old commands a squadron of older teens who sell crack cocaine. The Men's Group — open to the whole community — provides social support and self-development for dads who have been estranged from their families. And by working in tandem with mothers, it helps build bridges so men can reconnect with their children.*

### Background

St. Bernardine's Head Start was originally established in 1973 as the Glover-Tillman Learning Center, one of 10 Head Start programs in Baltimore. Since then it has grown from serving 27 children and their families to serving 200, has added a computer learning laboratory supported by IBM, and has developed a compre-

hensive adult education program for parents that offers classes in functional literacy, economic self-sufficiency, computer skills, family life, single parenting, training for the G.E.D., early childhood certification, and adult tutoring.

Under its dynamic director, Sheila Tucker, St. Bernardine's has also developed a set of principles that guides all activities, the Africentric Holistic Intergenerational Model. Each student is challenged to answer the question, "As an African-American, how do I empower myself and my family for productive living?" Each student is helped to develop his or her life as a whole person. And each is seen as part of a family experiencing a cycle of disadvantages, and taught how to break these cycles and instill a love of learning not only in their children, but in other family members.

According to Tucker, "Our philosophy is to empower the family, and you can't do that without looking at the role of the male. The welfare system disempowers the family by discouraging

**80**

the father from being any part of it, so women have to lie and say there's no male in the household. Agencies put data into the computers labeling us as single black female heads of households, totally misrepresenting the reality. In part, it was true that the mother was the primary caregiver, but there was no way we could ever start the process of healing and empowering the family without doing something meaningful and significant with the men."

## From Family Life Groups To The Men's Group

Actually doing something with the men at St. Bernardine's evolved from working with the women.

Sheila Tucker had always emphasized orientation for both parents — even though 90 percent of her families are female headed — "because both of them will be involved in some way in rearing the child. Even your uninvolved man is involved in some way. We know there will be needs for the mother."

But it was in the Family Life Groups, essentially weekly support groups for single moms, that the need to be more active with the men emerged. According to parent liaison Jacqueline Garner, "The women kept saying they were having difficulty in their relationships, difficulty with communicating or co-parenting. They had a lot of hostility toward the men. They'd say the father didn't need to be involved, that they

could raise their children just fine. We tried to help them understand that men play a key role in the growth of children, that unless the man is being abusive you need to build a relationship that will help support the child. We helped them see that even if he couldn't contribute financially, he could still take care of the children for a day, or be involved at the school, or talk to them on the phone."

"As we began the process of working with the women, we saw some of the anger going away. We saw the women stop alienating the men, stop using their anger as an excuse for him not to parent," says Sheila Tucker. "And the women started asking why couldn't there be something for their husbands or mates or the fathers of their children."

So the center began opening the Family Life Groups to men. "We were assuming that men didn't care," says Garner. "But when they came into the groups they started giving us a different perspective. But in a group of women most men are not going to feel safe enough to be open. The men needed their own group."

In 1986 and 1987, St. Bernardine's began offering a series of quarterly workshops, "The Black Male: Is He an Endangered Species?" There was a core group of guys who hung around to help develop it, informally called the Men's Group for want of a better name. When Clarence Tucker, Sheila's younger brother, joined the staff as a G.E.D. instructor in 1989,

**By sharing ideas, men become more comfortable around children.**

**The men's group has regular routines and rituals, including a closing ceremony.**

he took the leadership in expanding the Men's Group as a weekly part of the Head Start mental health component.

**Building Community**

"What united us in our first three months," says Clarence, "was finding out what we really wanted, finding a common goal that would attract and retain people. Everything kept coming back to community."

"A lot of Head Start Support Programs like family life, parenting, or communication look at building the individual. But if I go up to someone and say, 'You need to build communication skills or parenting skills,' they get defensive. But if I go up and say, 'Look at this community; we need to do something about it,' they agree. Our theme is that we're going to help community development through personal development."

Clarence began recruiting by hanging out on the corners, in the bars, in the social service lines, and in the neighborhood where men were doing menial jobs. "When you recruit one drug dealer he has some influence over at least five others. When you recruit one alcoholic, he has influence over five others. It doesn't matter if they are Head Start parents, though about 30 percent of ours are from St. Bernardine's and 10 percent are from other Head Start programs. If you can bring these people into the group, the word automatically starts getting around."

Get around it did. The Men's Group now includes about 35 men, with about a third of that number showing up on any one evening. And as it continues, its outreach builds.

To help design the program, Clarence and Sheila Tucker brought in two skilled profession-

als, psychologist Henry Gregory and adult education specialist Ademola Ekulona. In a female-dominated environment—24 out of 31 staff members are women—the design team found it had to stand up for men's needs. "We had a few rounds of vicious fighting to define the purpose," says Ekulona. "The women originally wanted the men's group to talk about feelings and communication and relationships because that's what they needed. I wasn't going to let them define a men's program on women's terms."

And Clarence wasn't about to include women in the group, even though the women's Family Life Group had been holding some sessions with men. "Having the women there might work when the men are more emotionally and financially secure," says Clarence. "We needed to target male parents and people who have influence on male parents. Right now most of these people are very vulnerable."

**Running the Group**

At 6:30 p.m. on a Wednesday night, three young men have already taken their places in the circle of chairs spread out in the classroom and are chatting with program leaders Clarence Tucker and Ademola Ekulona. Within a half-hour, eight more men ranging in age from 18 to 50 have drifted in, grabbing Clarence's hand and raising their hands to the group to signal "I'm here." Usually the group is led by Henry Gregory, but because he's in Atlanta for the evening, the call-to-order is made by Jerome who introduces himself and asks everybody to go around the circle and say their name and why they're here.

It is a big step for Jerome, a swarthy 48-year-old with only a few bottom teeth remaining on either side of his mouth. Consumed by alcoholism until recently, he has not held a job for 20 years. When he joined the Men's Group a year ago he would arrive from the street corner too intoxicated to complete a sentence. For Henry to have asked him to help Ademola and Clarence lead the discussion this week is a sign both of Jerome's progress and of the group's philosophy: empower by gradually assigning new responsibilities to the men whenever possible.

Several of the men have taken African names. A youth worker who wears a Dashiki top and black ivory carving around his neck says he comes to the group to keep in touch with himself and his community. Clarence, who boasts of being the only member never to have missed a meeting, says he comes to "stay grounded." Sam, who recently did 10 years of a 25-year sentence in jail for repeated drug trafficking and other crimes, announces that he's missed a few meetings but he's back. The first time he's asked his name and reason for attending, one gangly youth wipes tears away from his eyes, too choked up to speak. On the second round Neil Carr — recovering alcoholic, divorced father of three, a 31-year-old construction worker—says he is very glad to be here, that he's dealing with "a lot of hurt."

Though he says very little during the hour-long discussion, Neil says that the group has had a profound impact on him, and that he's always wanted it to meet more than once a week. "I listen to what the others say. I hear things I never would have thought of. I hear what other men are feeling and how they handle problems."

One of the principles of the Africentric model is to listen to the elders. Neil has listened to men 20 years his senior talk of their shame at failing their children, of using alcohol as a crutch. And he has listened to grown men talk about being accepted by their adult children, about making connections that had been absent for decades.

One of the greatest impacts of the group has been on Neil as a parent. His family situation is like a textbook case of the dilemmas of fatherhood among the black urban poor. Neil was married for eight years before separating from his wife, whose use of crack cocaine forced their split; he wanted her to stop, she called the police and accused him of hitting her, and the police threw him out of his home.

Neil swore to his wife that he wouldn't give her a penny because he knew it was just going for drugs. But he gives part of his salary every week to his wife's mother, who now cares for their four-year-old and three-month-old children. And he uses part of his salary to support his own mother, confined to the house with rheumatoid arthritis, who cares for Neil's seven-year-old son by a previous relationship.

Before joining the Men's Group, Neil didn't have much to do with his son. He went to work in the morning and then came home and went to sleep—or drank. "In the group I heard men talk about what they did with their children. I learned about rites of passage, about the importance of us taking care of our children." Now Neil says that every day after his construction job he helps his son with homework and is with him during the evening when he is not at AA meetings.

The two-hour meeting moves quickly. Before breaking for the hearty buffet dinner that follows every session—for many the best meal they will have all week—the men form a circle for the group's traditional closing ceremony. Arms

crossed in front, they clasp hands while reciting a mix of traditional Christian and African blessings, thanking the creator whose name is too long for anyone to pronounce.

### Bridging the Gap Between Men and Children

Sometimes helping men connect with their children means working with the mothers. For what the group brings to the surface is that some women are not letting the fathers see their children.

"The biggest issue," says Ademola Ekulona, "is if the man doesn't have the money, he doesn't see the child very often — the mother won't let him. He says, 'if she's going to give me that kind of hassle and demand something of me that I can't give, I'm going to wash my hands of it. I'm not going to beg and plead and lose my self respect.'

"So he washes his hands of the problem, but he doesn't wash the child out of his heart — and it hurts. We help him process that hurt so he can do something about it. If all she wants is money, then maybe he needs to explain what he's doing to get some. At the same time, I will let Sheila Tucker know that the mother is not letting him see the child, and try to arrange for him to spend some quality time with his child. In the Men's Group we emphasize the man's relationship with the child, regardless of his relationship with the mother."

### Contact

Clarence Tucker, Adult Education Coordinator
Sheila Tucker, Director
Al Brown, Parent Involvement Specialist
St. Bernardine's Head Start
3814 Edmondson Ave.
Baltimore, MD 21229
Phone: (410) 233-4500
Fax: (410) 362-6720

TIPS

- **Use a trained facilitator.** It doesn't have to be a psychologist, but a group leader needs to not only help men open up, but give them some tools they can use. He needs to help them move beyond negativity to something else.
- **Reward group members by giving them more responsibility.** Reward people for accomplishing, but don't knock them for not accomplishing. Give responsibility for helping prepare the meal and, after the group is established, let members run it instead of the psychologist.
- **Make adult education available.** Remember that in order to get jobs, people need skills.

Every week, the men meet to discuss their parenting problems and needs.

CHAPTER

# Reaching Men on the Move

## TEXAS MIGRANT COUNCIL

**Location:** Laredo, TX.
**Services:** 6,400 children

**Diversity:**
90% Mexican-American;
8-10% Anglo-American;
2-3% African-American

**Funding:** $17 million budget

*T*he Texas Migrant Council has a significant percentage of male staff at all levels and a high level of involvement from fathers in decision-making roles at the center and Policy Council levels. Fathers help organize the teams for sports competitions between neighborhood Head Start centers, work on fundraising barbecues, and plan and implement the Mr. and Miss Head Start Pageant.

### Background

The Texas Migrant Council is one of 28 Head Start grantees in the country that serves migrant workers. It serves over 5,000 children in 48 centers and home-based programs near the fields in Texas, then travels with families as they move from state to state, harvesting seasonal crops.

In a typical cycle the family travels in June from Texas to Minnesota to pick sugar beets for six or eight weeks. During July, August, and September they move to Indiana to pick tomatoes, eventually making their way to Florida for the harvesting of vegetables and citrus fruits. By October they have

returned to live and work in Texas. In 1991, the program traveled to Washington, Idaho, Wisconsin, Indiana, Ohio, and Kansas.

Head Start staff move in vans and buses with equipment for the program, while families use their own forms of transportation. Once on location, the day for children is geared to the picking schedule, 7 a.m. to 5 p.m., with families receiving all of the mandated services—bilingual education, health, and social services.

According to parent involvement social services coordinator Blas Reyes, men have been involved since the program began in 1971. "In our culture, it is unacceptable for women to travel alone. If women staff members or parents in the program have to travel it is expected that their spouses will travel along. Also the program required more men because of the need to have people strong enough to lift equipment that was being transported." Many men started as bus or van drivers but then stayed with the program to qualify themselves for teaching or other staff positions. In 1990, for example, over half of the

48 centers were directed by men; in 1991, of the 543 full- and part-time staff, 188 were men.

## Parents In Decision-Making Capacities

Typically, men hold four or five positions on the 20-plus member Parent Policy Council and one or more on the 10 person local parent advisory councils. Often they hold leadership positions.

Blas Reyes explains this relatively high level of participation as stemming from the early days of the program. In a typical scenario a father would wait in the truck outside the center with the younger children while the mother was inside attending a local parent meeting. Perhaps out of discomfort or curiosity, he would voice annoyance about being left outside, and staff would make it clear that he was welcome inside, too. He would take a look, get hooked on the program, and later become part of the decision-making parent committee.

In a variation on the same theme the father would complain that his wife was going on "fancy trips" to Albuquerque, New Mexico, for parent training. "How come she gets to go and I don't?" the father would ask. Reyes' answer would be, "If you want to go on trips, you have to get involved, like your wife!"

## Male Staff

Of the nearly 600 employees in the program, close to 80 percent are former migrant workers. Head Start salaries, low by comparison to outside standards, but high compared to migrant pay, are a big inducement for men. (Migrants still get close to minimum wage and often have to pay for their own lodging, travel to and from the camp, and food).

TMC's policy is to promote the involvement of males in all aspects of the program to serve as role models for the children and to influence male parents to get involved. Approximately one-third of the 300 teaching positions in 48 centers are held by men; half the central office and area supervisory staff are men; and almost all of the driver-custodians in the program are men.

## Barbecues, Sports, and Pageants

Parent involvement staff use a variety of inducements to get

men to participate. In Texas, according to Reyes, everyone likes barbecues and every poor person has a barbecue pit which uses readily available mesquite for fuel. Parents run barbecues for fund-raising events with the men usually doing the cooking.

TMC encourages sports contests between its' various centers. The men at the local programs usually set up the training for events such as relay races, with winners moving on to regional contests.

All centers have a Mr. and Miss Head Start pageant in which two of the children are chosen to represent the local center. Each involved family sells tickets to the event and this becomes a way of raising money for the Head Start program. The men of the program are very involved in all aspects of this activity.

## Parent Education

Because TMC life operates around the needs of the growers, Reyes and his staff keep in touch with the crew boss about the picking schedule. "No picking on Friday afternoon" becomes an opportunity to educate parents, especially the men, on such topics as the dangers of pesticides, regulations on crop spraying, new crops that are being planted in different sections of the country, legal aid, and wages. It is also a time when men are encouraged to come to classes to volunteer or fix up the Head Start center.

## Contact

Blas Reyes, Director
P.O. Box 2579
Laredo, TX 78044-2579
(210) 722-5174

---

**TIPS**

• **Involve men in physical activities such as fixing or building things at the center.** Male migrant workers live a very physical existence and carry this interest to the center.

• **Tap a man's talents.** Many men in TMC are skilled at playing the guitar, carpentry, plumbing, etc.

• **Bring in speakers.** Migrant workers are always interested in the legal and health issues affecting them.

• **Use sports to encourage involvement.** TMC has had men come to the center on a Saturday night to watch a televised sporting event and then stay for a short meeting.

Parents attended a dance at the center to watch their children participate.

# Resources

## Books for Children

The following books for preschoolers, featuring fathers, grandfathers, and other supportive male figures, also support multi-cultural curriculum development. General books are followed by books grouped according to race and ethnicity.

### General

*Ackerman, Karen.* **Song and Dance Man.** *Knopf, 1988.*
Grandpa, who was a song and dance man on a vaudeville stage, entertains his grandchildren.

*Andrews, Jon.* **The Auction.** *Macmillan, 1991.*
Sharing family memories helps comfort a boy and his grandfather when the family farm must be sold.

*Asch, Frank.* **Goodnight Horsey.** *Simon and Schuster, 1981.*
A little girl and her father pretend and share roles at bedtime.

*Aylesworth, Jim.* **Country Crossing.** *Atheneum, 1991.*
A grandfather and a small boy stop their old car on a country road in the middle of the night to watch the train go by.

*Barracca, Debra and Sal.* **The Adventures of Taxi Dog.** *Dial, 1990.*
Jim, the taxi driver, takes in a stray dog and together they take passengers all over the city.

*Baynton, Martin.* **Why Do You Love Me?** *Greenwillow, 1988.*
In the midst of a "why" age, a small boy tries to understand the love he and his father feel for each other.

*Blaine, Marge.* **The Terrible Thing That Happened at Our House.** *Four Winds, 1975.*
A girl feels no one has time to listen anymore when her mother gets a job. But father helps out and the family achieves a new understanding.

*Bradman, Tony.* **Not Like That, Like This!** *Oxford, 1988.*
An amusing counting book about the people who come to help when Dad's head gets stuck in the park railing. Dad is patient and good natured if not heroic.

*Browne, Anthony.* **Gorilla.** *Knopf, 1983.*
Hannah's father doesn't always give her the attention she needs but in the end she learns that he does care.

*Buckley, Helen E.* **Someday With My Father.** *Harper, 1985.*
A little girl dreams of the things she and her dad will do together—as soon as her cast comes off her leg.

*Bunting, Eve.* **Fly Away Home.** *Clarion, 1991.*
Homeless father and son living in the airport until they can find a home. Dad has some work on weekends. Older.

*Bunting, Eve.* **No Nap.** *Clarion, 1989.*
Dad is babysitting while mom is out, and a young girl refuses to take her nap.

*Bunting, Eve.* **A Perfect Father's Day.**
Father's Day is spent treating dad to all the things the child likes to do.

*Bunting, Eve.* **The Wall.** *Clarion, 1990.*
A boy and his father visit the Vietnam Veterans Memorial to find the name of the boy's grandfather, George Munoz.

*Burningham, John.* **Grandpa.** *Crown, 1985.*
A little girl and her grandfather share very special moments.

*Burningham, John.* **Mr. Gumpy's Outing.** *Holt, 1971.*
Mr. Gumpy's tolerant helpful kindness to his motley and misbehaving crew provides a model for good parenting. One of a series of Mr. Gumpy books.

*Burstein, Fred.* **Anna's Rain.** *Orchard, 1990.*
The birds need feeding even in the rain and a father helps his tiny daughter accomplish her mission.

*Burton, Virginia Lee.* **Mike Mulligan and His Steam Shovel.** *Houghton Mifflin, 1939.*
Mike Mulligan plays a fatherly role in his caring for his steam shovel, Mary Ann. Together they make an admirable team. An old favorite.

*Carlstrom, Nancy White.* **Grandpappy.** *Little Brown, 1990.*
A wise and loving grandfather shares experiences with his grandson when the boy comes to visit his home on the coast of Maine.

*Caseley, Judith.* **Grandpa's Garden Lunch.** *Greenwillow, 1990.*
Sarah and her Grandpa enjoy growing flowers and vegetables together. Then they share the fruits of their labor.

*Caseley, Judith.* **When Grandpa Came to Stay.** *Greenwillow, 1986.*
A boy helps his grandfather get used to life after his grandmother's death.

*Charney, Steve.* **Daddy's Whiskers.** *Crown, 1989.*
A rollicking song-story about the amazing uses for Daddy's long whiskers.

*Cole, Babette.* **The Trouble with Dad.** *Putnam's, 1985.*
The father in this amusing book is an inventor of robots.

*Cole, Sheila.* **When the Rain Stops.** *Lothrop, 1991.*
A small girl and her father share the pleasure of a sudden summer rain as they go out to gather blackberries.

*Day, Alexandra.* **Frank and Ernest.** *Scholastic, 1988.*
Two good friends (a bear and an elephant) do a great job running a diner while the owner is away. Special restaurant language adds to the appeal.

*Delton, Judy.* **A Walk on a Snowy Night.** *Harper, 1982.*
A walk in the country with dad on a snowy night. OP

*DePaolo, Tomie.* **Now One Foot, Now the Other.** *Putnam's, 1981.*
When he was tiny his grandfather helped Bobby learn to walk. After he has a stroke, it is Bobby who helps the grandfather walk again.

*DiSalvo-Ryan, DyAnne.* **Uncle Willie and the Soup Kitchen.** *Morrow, 1991.*
A sensitive and unsentimental picture book about a boy who helps his uncle, a regular volunteer at the soup kitchen. Older.

*Douglass, Barbara.* **Good as New.** *Lothrop, 1982.* When a bratty cousin destroys a young boy's favorite toy, Grandpa is able to fix it.

*Dupasquier, Phillipe.* **Dear Daddy.** *Bradbury Press, 1985.*
Sophie's father is away at sea but a strong presence in her thoughts. Pictures show his life in a strip above and Sophie's at home below.

*Eichler, Margaret.* **Martin's Father.** *Lollipop Power, 1971.*
Father and son run the household with efficiency and humor. Fun though the message is heavy. OP

*Friend, David.* **Baseball, Football, Daddy and Me.** *Viking, 1990.*
Each doublespread pictures a different sport and an excited youngster there with his father.

*Girard, Linda Walvoord.* **At Daddy's on Saturdays.** *Albert Whitman, 1987.*
A child of divorce spends time with her father.

*Goffstein, M.B.* **Two Piano Tuners.** *Farrar, Straus. 1977.*
This is the tale of a small girl who resolutely sticks to her desire to be a piano tuner like her grandfather rather than become the pianist he dreams she could be. Older.

*Greenberg, Melanie.* **My Father's Luncheonette.** *Dutton, 1991.*
A young girl's father welcomes her presence at his Bronx luncheonette. Autobiographical.

*Griffith, Helen.* **Georgia Music.** *Greenwillow, 1986.*
The songs of crickets and mocking birds accompany this gentle friendship between an old man and his granddaughter. The same two are together in Grandaddy's Place (Greenwillow, 1987).

*Haseley, Dennis.* **Kite Flier.** *Four Winds, 1986.*
Father and son grow up together, the father making marvelous kites for his son. Finally the son must separate and go his way and the father makes one last magnificent kite. Older. OP

*Hazen, Barbara Shook.* **Tight Times.** *Viking, 1983.*
When a boy's father loses his job, tight times set in - but family love alleviates the situation.

*Hazen, Barbara Shook.* **Two Homes to Live In: A Child's Eye View of Divorce.** *Human Sciences Press, 1978.*
A young child's changing adjustment to the divorce of loved parents, told in the honest voice of young childhood.

*Hendershot, Judith.* **In Coal Country.** *Knopf, 1987.*
The recollections of a childhood growing up in a company town include a strong father who was proud of his work in the mines.

*Henkes, Kevin.* **Grandpa and Bo.** *Greenwillow, 1986.*
Young Bo spends the summer with Grandfather, and has a wonderful time.

*Hest, Amy.* **The Crack-of-Dawn Walkers.** *Macmillan, 1984.*
Every other Sunday a young girl and her grandfather go on their special walk together.

*Hines, Anna Grossnickle.* **Daddy Makes the Best Spaghetti.** *Clarion, 1986.*
Daddy is the primary caretaker while mom works.

*Hoban, Russell.* **Bedtime for Frances.** *Harper, 1960.*
An impish badger pulls the usual childish delaying tactics but gives in when father uses that "special voice"!

*James, Betsy.* **Natalie Underneath.** *Dutton, 1990.*
A young girl and her little brother have a wonderful time exploring underneath things around the house as their

patient father watches over them.

*Jones, Carol.* **This Old Man.** *Houghton, Mifflin, 1990.*
The pictures for this charming version of a favorite nursery song show the old man who plays nick nack to be a grandfather.

*Kirk, Barbara.* **Grandpa, Me, and Our House in the Tree.** *Macmillan, 1978.*
Even though grandpa becomes very ill he can still help Nico make a tin can telephone for his tree house. OP

*Lasky, Kathryn.* **I Have Four Names for My Grandfather.** *Little Brown, 1976.*
Fine photos highlight the close relationship of a young boy and his grandfather.

*Lewis, Kim.* **The Shepherd Boy.** *Four Winds, 1990.*
Through the year James watches his shepherd father at work and at the end they go off to the fields together.

*Lobel, Arnold.* **Mouse Tales.** *Harper, 1972.*
Seven funny, original, imaginative stories told by Poppa Mouse to his seven mouse boys.

*Lobel, Arnold.* **Uncle Elephant.** *Harper, 1981.*
When a small elephant's parents are lost, his uncle cares for him with tender understanding and love until the happy ending reunites the family.

*Long, Earlene.* **Gone Fishing.** *Houghton, Mifflin, 1984.*
A little boy and his father go on a fishing trip, "a big fish for daddy...a little fish for me".

Lyon, George. **Cecil's Story.** Orchard, 1991.
A boy waits for his father, "a man strong enough to lift you with just one arm," to come home, injured, from the Civil War.

McClosky, Robert. **One Morning in Maine.** Viking, 1952.
The delights of clam digging, fooling with boats, and losing teeth in the company of a laid-back laconic dad.

McPhail, David. **Ed and Me.** Harcourt, 1990.
Ed is an old pick up truck, and a small girl and her farmer father are united in their affection for it.

Minarik, Else. **Father Bear Comes Home.** Harper, 1959.
The very young child identifies with Little Bear's excited happiness while waiting for Father Bear. (One of a series).

Ness, Evaline. **Sam, Bangs, and Moonshine.** Holt, 1966.
A fisherman father tries to keep his daughter from tall-tale telling; when a tragedy is barely averted, instead of deepening her guilt, he offers her an understanding solution. Older.

Ormerod, Jan. **Dad's Back.** Lothrop, 1985.
Dad comes home and plays with baby. Messy Baby, Reading and Sleeping are also about fathers and babies.

Otey, Mimi. **Daddy Has a Pair of Striped Shorts.** Farrar, Straus, 1990.
A girl realizes people seem to like her caring father even if he does dress outlandishly.

Oxenbury, Helen. **Tom and Pippo Read a Story.** Aladdin, 1988.
A boy and his toy monkey enjoy having daddy read to them. For the youngest.

Parker, Kristy. **My Dad the Magnificent.** Dutton, 1987.
An amusing story about a little boy whose ordinary Saturday routines with his dad are just as great as if his father really was a lion tamer or a dog sled driver.

Perry, Patricia and Marietta Lynch. **Mommy and Daddy Are Divorced.** Dial, 1978.
Father's Saturday visits are important to his two small sons in this photo-story about divorce.

Pomerantz, Charlotte. **Timothy Tall Feather.** Greenwillow, 1986.
A boy and his grandfather tell a joint story about Indians.

Porte, Barbara. **Harry's Dog.** Greenwillow, 1984.
Harry's father is very supportive even though he is allergic to Harry's dog. In Harry's Mom (Greenwillow, 1985) the patience and humor of Harry's father, a single parent, is again demonstrated. Harry Gets an Uncle (Greenwillow, 1991) features an interracial band with Harry's Aunt Rose on piano.

Quinlan, Patricia. **My Dad Takes Care of Me.** Annick Press, 1987.
An out-of-work father takes a correspondance course and also cares for his son.

Rice, Eve. **Papa's Lemonade.** Greenwillow, 1976.
Papa has pennies in his pocket and knows how to make lemonade out of oranges. OP

Richardson, Jean. **Thomas's Sitter.** Four Winds, 1991.
The babysitter for Thomas and his infant sister turns out to be Don, a young man who really understands what a pre-school boy feels like.

Rockwell, Anne. **Handy Hank Will Fix It.** Holt, 1988.
From plumbing to plastering, it's all in a day's work for Hank.

Roy, Ron. **Breakfast With My Father.** Clarion, 1980.
A boy's delight in continuing attentions of his divorced father has a new twist to the resolution. Touching incidents between a man and his child. OP

Rylant, Cynthia. **All I See.** Orchard, 1988.
A friendship grows between a boy and the young artist who paints beside the lake.

Seuss, Dr. **Horton Hatches an Egg.** Random, 1940.
"An elephant's faithful one hundred percent," says the clumsy Horton as he crouches day and night on an egg he promised to keep warm.

Shannon, George. **The Piney Woods Peddler.** Greenwillow, 1981.
A peddler goes trading to get a silver dollar for his dear darling daughter in this charming version of an Appalachian folk tale.

Stecher, Miriam B. and Alice S. Kandell. **Daddy and Ben Together.** Lothrop, 1981.
A small boy and his father have a close time together while mother is away.

Steig, William. **Sylvester and the Magic Pebble.** Farrar, Straus, 1969.
His father and mother's deep love helps break the enchantment Sylvester, the donkey, has unwittingly brought on himself. A favorite Steig fable.

Stevenson, James. **Could Be Worse!** Greenwillow, 1977.
The first in a series of wonderful tales told by a loving grandpa to his two grandchildren.

Sutherland, Harry A. **Dad's Car Wash.** Atheneum, 1988.
The young boy is the car, and the tub is Dad's car wash.

Townsend, Maryann and Ronnie Stern. **Pop's Secret.** Addison-Wesley, 1980.
Warm relationships between child and grandfather. The many photographs of how people looked in the earlier decades of the century will satisfy young children's curiosity.

Wantanabe, Shigeo. **Daddy, Play With Me!.** Philomel, 1984.
"I love to play with Daddy," says Little Bear, star of a favorite series of books for toddlers.

Williams, Vera. **More, More, More Said the Baby.** Greenwillow, 1990.
"More, more, more," laughs Little Guy when his father kisses him on the belly button in the first of three love stories between grown-ups and children.

Yolen, Jane. **Owl Moon.** Philomel, 1987. A father and his young daughter go out late on a cold winter's night to talk to owls.

Yorinks, Arthur. **Hey, Al.** Farrar, Straus, 1986.
A modern city fable about an affectionate janitor and his dog who discovers that "paradise lost is sometimes Heaven found."

### African-American

Adoff, Arnold. **Hard to Be Six.** Lothrop, 1991.
Interracial family. Dad is sympathetic to boy's "younger brother" struggles.

Adoff, Arnold. **In for Winter, Out for Spring.** Harcourt, 1991.
Becka belongs in her home with Mom, Dad, and brother Aaron. Poems and pictures portray a father who is strong and caring.

Appiah, Sonia. **Amoko and Efua Bear.** Macmillan, 1988.
In a story set in Ghana, Amoko's father not only takes her to market and lets her help him cook, he finds her beloved toy bear when it is missing.

Bang, Molly. **The Paper Crane.** Greenwillow, 1985.
A kind stranger with a paper crane that becomes real helps a man and his son save their tiny restaurant.

Barrett, Joyce. **Willie's Not the Hugging Kind.** Harper, 1989.
Reacting to a friend's teasing, Willie refuses to be hugged until he realizes how much he misses this expression of love from his family, including his father.

Barton, Byron. **Machines at Work.** Crowell, 1987. Barton's bold child-like drawings show workers of both sexes and a variety of colors as they bulldoze, dig, load, mix, dump and build. Children also like Airplanes, Trucks (Crowell, 1986) and I Want to Be an Astronaut (Crowell, 1988).

Breinburg, Petronella. **Shawn's Red Bike.** Crowell, 1976.
Patrick's dad and uncle Fred help Shawn save money for his new bike and a big boy helps him start learning to ride. OP

Caines, Jeanette. **Daddy.** Harper, 1977.
A small daughter of divorced parents loves Saturdays with her dad; their relationship isn't weakened though their time together is shortened.

Caines, Jeanette. **I Need a Lunch Box.** Harper, 1988.
A younger brother is jealous of his older sister getting ready for school. Father helps solve the problem.

Cameron, Ann. **The Stories Julian Tells.** Pantheon, 1981.
A wonderful and surprising father sparks his child's imagination into the creation of original and amusing stories. Good for reading aloud to children 5 and up.

Clifton, Lucille. **Amifika.** Dutton, 1977.
A young boy is afraid he is one of the things "that will have to go" to make room for his returning soldier father. His father's love reassures him. OP

Clifton, Lucille. Everett **Anderson's Goodbye.** Holt, 1983.
A young boy goes through the stages of grief for his dad who loves him "through and through."

Clifton, Lucille. **My Friend Jacob.** Dutton, 1980.
Jacob, an older mentally retarded boy, is a generous and caring friend to his next door neighbor, Sam. Pictures show Jacob to be white and Sam brown skinned. OP

Cummings, Pat. **Jimmy Lee Did It.** Lothrop, 1985.
A sister-brother story in rhyme shows the father making pancakes.

Dragonwagon, Crescent. **Half a Moon and One Whole Star.** Macmillan, 1986.
While Susan sleeps a sailor, a saxophone player, and a baker ply their trades.

Feelings, Muriel. **Jambo Means Hello: Swahili Alphabet Book.** Dial, 1974.
Craftsmen, teachers, drummers, healers and harvesters are some of the men pictured in this attractive alphabet book. Another book by the same author and illustrator is Moja Means One: Swahili Counting Book (Dial 1971).

George, Jean Craighead. **The Wentletrap Trap.** Dutton, 1978.
On the island of Bimini a conch fisherman encourages his son to look for a rare seashell. OP

Greenfield, Eloise. **First Pink Light.** Crowell, 1976.
A small boy wants to stay up and greet his father who is returning home just before dawn. OP

Greenfield, Eloise. **Grandpa's Face.** *Philomel, 1988.* Grandpa's wonderful ever changing face always shows love when he looks at his granddaughter, Tamika.

Greenfield, Eloise. **Nathaniel Talking.** *Black Butterfly Children's Books, 1988.* Although Nathaniel is a little older, pre-schoolers will enjoy some of the poems like "My Daddy" as well as the large soft black and white drawings.

Gray, Genevieve. **Send Wendell.** *McGraw-Hill, 1974.* An uncle visiting from California becomes a special friend for a six year old. OP

Hanft, Philip. **Never Fear, Flip the Dip Is Here.** *Dial, 1991.* Flip learns to really catch and throw a baseball when Buster, the artist, becomes his coach. Interracial.

Hayes, Sarah. **Eat Up Gemma.** *Lothrop, 1988.* Mom, Dad and Grandma all try to get baby Gemma to eat but it's her big brother that succeeds.

Heide, Florence. **The Day of Ahmed's Secret.** *Lothrop, 1990.* Ahmed's father has taught him how to find his way through the streets of Cairo where he delivers bottles of fuel from his donkey cart.

Hort, Lenny. **How Many Stars in the Sky?** *Tambourine Books, 1991.* With Mom away, both a boy and his father have trouble sleeping so they go on an all night star counting drive.

Howard, Elizabeth. **Chita's Christmas Tree.** *Bradbury, 1989.* Not only Papa, but the waffleman and many loving uncles are part of a little girl's Christmas in early 20th century Baltimore.

Hughes, Shirley. **The Big Concrete Lorry.** *Lothrop, 1990.* All the men in the neighborhood help Dad lay the foundation for the extension he's adding to the family's overcrowded house.

Johnson, Angela. **When I Am Old With You.** *Orchard, 1990.* A child imagines all the comforting and pleasant things to do with Gradaddy if they were old together.

Johnson, Herschel. **A Visit to the Country.** *Harper, 1989.* Grandpa and Mike like to watch the trains go by and it's Grandpa who finds a cage for Mike's bird. Pictures by the African-American artist, Romare Bearden.

Joseph, Lynn. **Coconut Kind of Day.** *Lothrop, 1990.* These short poems from Trinidad recall "coconut drives with daddy," a big brother who is an accomplished swimmer and the men who sell mangoes and ice cream in the streets.

Keats, Ezra Jack. **Peter's Chair.** *Harper, 1967.* Peter finds it easier to get used to the new baby when his father helps him repaint his outgrown chair for her.

Levin, Hugh. **Jafta's Father.** *Carolrhoda, 1983.* One of four books set in South Africa, this one is a tribute to Jafta's father "as tall and strong as a tree."

Lexau, Joan. **Me Day.** *Dial, 1971.* Rafe's birthday doesn't look promising until his divorced father makes a surprise visit. OP

Mandelbaum, Phil. **You Be Me, I'll Be You.** *Kane Miller, 1990.* An interracial family with a white father and a brown daughter who wants to look like her father. Flour, coffee grounds and braids help them see each other and themselves in a new way.

Moppel, Tolowa. **The Orphan Boy.** *Clarion, 1990.* In this beautifully illustrated Masai legend of the planet Venus, a lonely old man welcomes the sudden appearance of an orphan boy.

Morris, Ann. **Loving.** *Lothrop, 1990.* Strong color photographs and simple text show fathers, among others, from all over the world caring for their children.

Nolan, Madeena. **My Daddy Don't Go to Work.** *Carolrhoda, 1978.* A realistic story about a father discouraged about finding a job. For the child he is still a good father. Older. OP

*Williams, Vera. **Cherries and Cherry Pits.** Greenwillow, 1986.*
Bidemmi loves to draw. One of her pictures is of a father bringing cherries home to his children and another is of a big brother who brings a cherry to his sister.

### Asian-American

*Bang, Molly. **Ten, Nine, Eight.** Greenwillow, 1983.*
A father puts his little daughter to bed in a warm and comfortable setting.

*Behrens, June. **Soo Ling Finds a Way.** Golden Gate Junior Books, 1965.* How Soo Ling's grandfather takes the magic of his iron to the new laundromat. OP

*Ringgold, Faith. **Tar Beach.** Crown, 1991.*
Daddy, a construction worker, is a strong presence in this beautifully magical dream story of city child, Cassie.

*Seeger, Pete. **Abiyoyo.** Macmillan, 1986.*
Based on a South African lullaby and folk story. A boy who plays the ukulele and a father who makes things disappear with his magic wand team up to rid the town of the terrible giant.

*Shelby, Anne. **We Keep a Store.** Orchard, 1990.*
"You all come back" the father says to the people that visit the family's tiny country store.

*Spohn, David. **Winter Wood.** Lothrop, 1991.*
Matt and his Dad split and carry wood for their stove on a cold winter day. Pictures show an interracial family.

*Steptoe, John. **Baby Says.** Lothrop, 1988.*
It takes patience for older brother to play with the baby.

*Steptoe, John. **Daddy Is a Monster...Sometimes.** J.B. Lippincott, 1980.*
Daddy is only a monster when he's got monster kids. Other times he's really in there being a good Dad.

*Steptoe, John. **My Special Best Words.** Viking, 1974.*
A young father's good relationship with his two children. The "bathroom talk" may be offensive to some but will appeal to others. OP

*Stolz, Mary. **Storm In the Night.** Harper, 1986.*
A grandfather helps a boy know it's all right to be afraid sometimes.

*Thomas, Ianthe. **Eliza's Daddy.** Harcourt Brace, 1976.*
Eliza wonders and worries about her divorced daddy's new family, especially the new daughter. But on meeting her, Eliza's fears vanish. OP

*Thomas, Ianthe. **Willie Blows a Mean Horn.** Harper, 1981.*
An admiring relationship between a boy and his jazz musician father in a realistic Harlem setting.

*Udry, Janice. **What Mary Jo Shared.** A. Whitman, 1966.*
A shy child has trouble with show and tell until she decides to share her father with the class.

*Walter, Mildred Pitts. **Ty's One-Man Band.** Four Winds, 1980.*
Andro, the peglegged one-man band, doesn't disappoint Ty. He really makes music with washboard, spoons, comb, and pail.

*Friedman, Ina. **How My Parents Learned to Eat.** Houghton Mifflin, 1984.*
An amusing story of how an American sailor learns to eat with chopsticks and his Japanese wife-to-be with a knife and fork.

*Say, Allen. **The Lost Lake.** Houghton Mifflin, 1989.*
A single parent father and his young son have trouble reaching each other until they go camping together and discover their own "lost lake." A picture book for older children.

*Stock, Catherine. **Emma's Dragon Hunt.** Lothrop, 1984.*
Grandfather Wang, newly arrived from China, explains dragon lore to his fortunate granddaughter.

Tompert, Ann. *Grandfather Tang's Story.* Crown, 1990. Gradfather Tang and Little Soo are playing a game with their Chinese tongrams, shifting the shapes into different animals as they tell a story.

Wallace, Ian. *Chin Chiang and the Dragon's Dance.* Atheneum, 1984. How a young Chinese-American boy gains enough confidence to dance in the tail of his grandfather's dragon.

Yashima, Taro. *Umbrella.* Viking, 1967. Father comes to take three-year-old Momo home from nursery school and walks with her while she uses her new umbrella.

Yolen, Jane. *The Emperor and the Kite.* Philomel, 1988. In the end it is the smallest and most insignificant daughter who helps her father, the Emperor, escape from his prison tower and sits beside him on the throne.

*Entries with an OP notation are out of print.*

## Hispanic
Brown, Tricia. *Hello, Amigos!* Holt, 1986. A photographic essay shows a Mexican-American family gathering for a boy's birthday fiesta. At the end, father and child walk to church to light a candle together.

Lomas, Garza, Carmen. *Family Pictures. Cuadros de Familia.* Children's Book Press, 1990. Memories of growing up in Kingsville, Texas near the border with Mexico. Fathers and grandfathers are an important part of the many good times shared by the artist's family. In English and Spanish.

Politi. Leo. *Song of the Swallows.* Scribners, 1949, 1986. Juan's best friend is old Julian, the bell ringer and gardener at the Capistrano Mission.

Roe, Eileen. *Com Mi Hermano / With My Brother.* Bradbury, 1991. Pictures and text in two languages portray the warm relationship between a high school aged boy and his pre-school brother.

Rohmer, Harriet. *Uncle Nacho's Hat: El Sombrero del tio Nacho.* Children's Book Press, 1989. How Ambrosia gets a new hat for her lovable uncle. In English and Spanish.

Sonneborn, Ruth. *Friday Night Is Papa Night.* Viking, 1970, 1987. A small Puerto Rican boy waits and waits with sure faith that his beloved Papa will make it home as usual on Friday night.

## Native American and Inuit
Cleaver, Elizabeth. *The Enchanted Caribou.* Atheneum, 1985. Etosack, a young Inuit man, rescues Tyya when enchantment turns her into a white caribou. An old tale which can be made into a shadow puppet and play.

Hertz, Ole. *Tobias Has a Birthday.* Carolrhoda, 1981. Father hoists the flag because it is Tobias's birthday. A family in Greenland celebrates together. More about Tobias and his family in Tobias Catches Trout and Tobias Goes Seal Hunting. Small books by a cultural anthropologist.

Jeffers, Susan. *Brother Eagle, Sister Sky: A Message from Chief Seattle.* Dial, 1991. Chief Seattle pleads for the connectedness of man and nature in a poetic book which pictures many strong male figures.

Martin, Bill. *Knots on a Counting Rope.* Holt, 1987. As he repeats the story of the boy's life and of his courage and skill, a wise grandfather helps his blind grandson to grow in self-confidence.

# Materials for Professionals and Parents
These books, articles, and other print resources will help you think further about male involvement. Materials about fathers are followed by materials about men in early childhood education.

## Materials About Fathers
### ■ Popular
These are good resources to have in your library for parents and staff.

Louv, R. (1993). Father Love: What We Need, What We Seek, What We Must Create. New York: Pocket Books.

Pruett, K. (1987). The Nurturing Father. New York: Warner Books.

Shapiro, J. (1993). The Measure of a Man: Becoming the Father You Wish Your Father Had Been. New York: Delacorte.

Sullivan, S. Adams. (1992). The Father's Almanac. New York: Doubleday.

### ■ Professional
These are good resources in case you want to dig deeper into the research on fatherhood and male involvement.

Biller, H. (1971). Father, Child, & Sex Role. Lexington, MA: Heath.

Bozett, F. & S. Hanson, Eds. (1991). Fatherhood and Families in Cultural Context. New York, NY: Springer.

Bronstein, P. & Cowan, C.P. (1988). Fatherhood Today: Men's Changing Role in the Family. New York: Wiley.

Gary, L., Beatty, L, & Weaver, G. (1987). Involvement of Black Fathers in Head Start (Final report submitted to the Department of Health and Human Services, ACYF, Grant No. 90-CD-0509). Washington, D.C.: Institute for Urban Affairs and Research, Ho

Hanson, S., & Bozett, F., Eds. (1985). Dimensions in Fatherhood. Beverly Hills, CA: Sage Publications.

Klinman, D.G., Kohl, R., & The Fatherhood Project (1984). Fatherhood U.S.A. New York, NY: Garland Publishing, Inc.

Klinman, D.G. & Sander, J. (1985). Reaching and Serving the Teenage Father. New York: Bank Street College of Education.

Lamb, M.E. & Sagi, A., Eds. (1983). Fatherhood and Family Policy. Hillsdale, N.J.: Erlbaum.

Lamb, M.E., Ed. (1991). The Father's Role: Applied Perspectives. New York, NY: John Wiley & Sons.

Lamb, M.E., Ed. (1987). The Father's Role: Cross-cultural Perspectives. Hillsdale, N.J.: Erlbaum.

Lamb, M.E., Ed. (1986). The Role of the Father in Child Development (2nd edition). New York, NY: John Wiley & Sons.

Levine, J.A. (1975). Who Will Raise the Children? New Options for Fathers (and Mothers). New York: J.B. Lippincott.

Miedzian, M. (1991). Boys Will Be Boys: Breaking the Link Between Masculinity and Violence. New York: Doubleday.

Powell, D.R. (1989). Families and Early Childhood Programs. Washington, DC: NAEYC.

Robinson, B. (1988). Teenage Fathers. Lexington, MA: Lexington Books.

**Curricula**
Betterman, G. (1984). Fathering. White Bear Lake, MN: Minnesota Curriculum Services Center.

Meyer, D.J., Vadasy, P.F., Fewell, R.R., & Schell, G.C. (1985). A Handbook for the Fathers' Program. Seattle, WA: University of Washington Press.

Palm, G., Johnson, L., & The Minnesota Fathering Allliance. (1992). Working with Fathers: Methods and Perspectives. Stillwater, MN: Nu Ink Unlimited.

**Materials About Men in Early Childhood Education**
■ **Books and Chapters in Books**
Nelson, B. & Sheppard, B., Eds. (1992). Men in Child Care & Early Education: A Handbook for Administrators & Educators. Minneapolis, MN: Men in Child Care Project, 2420 31st Avenue South, Minneapolis, MN 55406.

Seifert, K. (1987). Men in Early Childhood Education. B. Spodek , D. Peters, & O. Saracho (Eds.). Professionalism in Early Childhood Education. 105-116. New York, NY: Teachers College Press, Columbia University.

■ **Articles**
Cohen, D.L. (Nov/Dec 1990). Looking For a Few Good Men: Why Are There So Few Male Teachers in the Early Grades? Education Week, 2(3), 14-15.

Costello, J. (Nov. 1979). When Men Teach Young Children. Parents Magazine.

Giveans, D.L. (March/April 1991). Men in Child Care: An Important Minority. Early Childhood News, 3, (2).

Gold, D., & Reis, M. (1982). Male Teacher Effects On Young Children: A Theoretical and Empirical Consideration. Sex Roles, 8, 493-513.

Lee, P., & Wolinsky, A. (Aug. 1973). Male Teachers of Young Children: A Preliminary Study. Young Children.

Levine, J.A. (May 1978). "Explaining" About Men and Young Children. Young Children, 33(4), 14-15.

May, C. (April 1971). Men Teachers in Early Childhood Education: Which Direction Will They Take Now? Contemporary Education.

Robinson, B. (1981). Changing Views on Male Early Education Teachers. Young Children, 36(5), 27-32.

Robinson, B. (1979). Men Caring for The Young: An Androgynous Perspective. The Family Coordinator, 553-560.

Robinson, B., & Canaday, H. (1978). Sex-role Behaviors & Personality Traits of Male Day Care Teachers. Sex Roles, 4, (6).

Robinson, B., Skeen, P. Flake, C. (Sept./Oct. 1980). Sex-role: Contributions of Male Teachers in Early Education Settings. Early Childhood.

Robinson, B., Skeen, P., & Coleman, M. (1984). Professionals' Attitudes Towards Men in Early Childhood Education: A national study. Children and Youth Services Review, 6, 101-113.

Robinson, B.E. (Sept. 1988). Vanishing Breed: Men in Child Care Programs. Young Children.

Seifert, K. (1973). Some Problems of Men in Child Care Center Work. Child Welfare. 52 (3), 167-171.

Williams, B. (1970). Of Hairy Arms & a Deep Baritone Voice: A Symposium Men in Young Children's Lives. Childhood Education, 47, 139-143.

## Organizations
Contact the following organizations and programs involving fathers and other men for information, support, and networking.

The Fatherhood Project
Families and Work Institute
330 Seventh Avenue
New York, NY 10001
(212) 465-2044
Contact: James A. Levine

Men's Issues Think Tank
4839 305th Avenue, N.E.
Cambridge, MN 55008
(612) 689-5885
Contact: Lowell Johnson

Men in Child Care
2420 31st Avenue (South)
Minneapolis, MN 55406
(612) 724-3430
Contact: Bryan Nelson

National Center for Family-Centered Care
7910 Woodmont Avenue, Suite 300
Betheseda, MD. 20814
(301) 654-6549
Contact: James May, Editor, National Fathers Network Newsletter

# About This Book

In researching this book, we used a combination of techniques to identify programs that exemplified successful approaches to male involvement. First, we sent mailings to every local affiliate of the National Association for the Education of Young Children (NAEYC), every member of the National Association of Child Care Resource and Referral Agencies (NACCR-RA), every regional office of Head Start, and an assortment of sympathetic researchers throughout the country. We then made follow-up telephone calls to many of these organizations. Bit by bit, one group would lead us to another that was doing interesting work. Soon we had a pool of over twenty programs to interview in depth by telephone. Out of those we selected thirteen for on-site visits where, over the course of several days, we observed programs in action and interviewed parents and staff—in each case both males and females.

We concentrated our search on programs serving low-income families, since they present the greatest concern for social policy. We sought a distribution comprised half of Head Start programs and half of other types of early childhood programs, again for social policy reasons: Head Start, more than any other program, is poised for expansion. It is a program in which it may be possible to have an especially important impact. Subsequent to the launch of our project, Head Start began attending to—and allocating dollars for—ways to increase male involvement. This was part of a Male Involvement Initiative instigated by the Secretary of Health and Human Services, Dr. Louis Sullivan. We have been able to serve as consultants to the Administration for Children and Families and the Head Start Bureau on that initiative.

Despite our emphases on Head Start and other low-income programs, we did attend to middle-income programs and have included profiles of two programs, Dad and Me in Minnesota and Parents as Teachers in Missouri, that operate without regard to parental income. Moreover, most of the lessons learned in our research will be valuable to all programs.

When we started our search, we did not have a fixed definition of father involvement in mind. We did, of course, have areas to question about and a range of criteria, but in general we were looking for programs that were doing something interesting, something that might be replicated or applied elsewhere. It didn't have to be a comprehensive program for males, but we ruled out "one shots," programs that made a claim to involvement because they hosted one annual event for fathers or other men. We were looking for programs with more breadth, depth and staying power.

In each community where we located an exemplary program, we also visited a program serving a comparable population that wasn't successfully involving males. We wanted to make sure that involvement wasn't a factor of the population served, and to better highlight the strategies used by the successful programs. The research process was one of discovery for us, and we expect this book to be one of discovery for you too.

# About the Authors

**James A. Levine** is director of The Fatherhood Project at the Families and Work Institute in New York City. He has worked with, and for, children as a preschool teacher, day care director, founding director of the national School-Age Child Care Project, and vice president of the Bank Street College of Education. The author of five books and scores of articles for professional and popular audiences, Levine appears frequently on television, radio, and in the press as an expert on families and children.

**Dennis T. Murphy, Ph.D.**, is an associate professor with the Graduate Department of Educational Leadership and Administration at the C.W. Post campus of Long Island University. A former teacher, Head Start director, and public school and college administrator, he writes extensively for a variety of educational journals. Murphy is a facilitator of men's groups and consultant to school districts and not-for-profit agencies.

**Sherrill Wilson, Ph.D.**, is an urban anthropologist who currently directs the Liaison Office of the African Burial Grounds and Five Points Archaeological Project in New York City, based on the excavation of the largest African burial ground in the United States. She also operates a Black History tour business. Wilson has conducted many studies of social and educational services, receiving her doctorate from the New School for Social Research.